Slowing Down

Slowing Down

GEORGE MELLY

Drawings by Maggi Hambling

VIKING
an imprint of
PENGUIN BOOKS

VIKING

Published by the Penguin Group
Penguin Books Ltd, 80 Strand, London WC2R ORL, England
Penguin Group (USA) Inc., 375 Hudson Street, New York, New York 10014, USA
Penguin Group (Canada), 90 Eglinton Avenue East, Suite 700, Toronto, Ontario, Canada M4P 2Y3
(a division of Pearson Penguin Canada Inc.)
Penguin Ireland, 25 St Stephen's Green, Dublin 2, Ireland
(a division of Penguin Books Ltd)
Penguin Group (Australia), 250 Camberwell Road,
Camberwell, Victoria 3124, Australia (a division of Pearson Australia Group Pty Ltd)
Penguin Books India Pvt Ltd, 11 Community Centre,
Panchsheel Park, New Delhi – 110 017, India
Penguin Group (NZ), cnr Airborne and Rosedale Roads, Albany,
Auckland 1310, New Zealand (a division of Pearson New Zealand Ltd)
Penguin Books (South Africa) (Pty) Ltd, 24 Sturdee Avenue,
Rosebank, Johannesburg 2196, South Africa

Penguin Books Ltd, Registered Offices: 80 Strand, London WC2R ORL, England

www.penguin.com

First published 2005
2

Copyright © George Melly, 2005

The moral right of the author has been asserted

'The Old Fools' from *Collected Poems* by Philip Larkin, reprinted by permission of Faber & Faber.
'Musée des Beaux Arts' and 'Secrets' from *Collected Poems* by W. H. Auden,
reprinted by permission of Faber & Faber.
'East Coker III' from *Four Quartets* by T. S. Eliot, reprinted by permission of Faber & Faber.
Surrealist Games, edited by Mel Gooding, reprinted by permission of Redstone Press,
7a St Lawrence Terrace, London W10 5SU. http://www.redstonepress.co.uk/

Drawings of George Melly by Maggi Hambling, copyright © Maggi Hambling

Set in 13.5/16pt Monotype Garamond
Typeset by Rowland Phototypesetting Ltd, Bury St Edmunds, Suffolk
Printed in Great Britain by Clays Ltd, St Ives plc

A CIP catalogue record for this book is available from the British Library

ISBN 0-670-91409-6

To most of my family and all my true friends

Contents

1. Old Fools' Time

The Old Fools

What do they think has happened, the old fools,
To make them like this? Do they somehow suppose
It's more grown-up when your mouth hangs open and
    drools,
And you keep on pissing yourself, and can't remember
Who called this morning? Or that, if they only chose,
They could alter things back to when they danced all
    night,
Or went to their wedding, or sloped arms some
    September?
Or do they fancy there's really been no change,
And they've always behaved as if they were crippled or tight,
Or sat through days of thin continuous dreaming
Watching light move? If they don't (and they can't) it's
    strange:
    Why aren't they screaming?

At death, you break up: the bits that were you
Start speeding away from each other for ever
With no one to see. It's only oblivion, true:
We had it before, but then it was going to end,
And was all the time merging with a unique endeavour
To bring to bloom the million-petalled flower

Slowing Down

Of being here. Next time you can't pretend
There'll be anything else. And these are the first signs:
Not knowing how, not hearing who, the power
Of choosing gone. Their looks show that they're for it:
Ash hair, toad hands, prune face dried into lines –
    How can they ignore it?

Perhaps being old is having lighted rooms
Inside your head, and people in them, acting.
People you know, yet can't quite name; each looms
Like a deep loss restored, from known doors turning,
Setting down a lamp, smiling from a stair, extracting
A known book from the shelves; or sometimes only
The rooms themselves, chairs and a fire burning,
The blown bush at the window, or the sun's
Faint friendliness on the wall some lonely
Rain-ceased midsummer evening. That is where they live:
Not here and now, but where all happened once.
    This is why they give

An air of baffled absence, trying to be there
Yet being here. For the rooms grow farther, leaving
Incompetent cold, the constant wear and tear
Of taken breath, and them crouching below
Extinction's alp, the old fools, never perceiving
How near it is. This must be what keeps them quiet:
The peak that stays in view wherever we go
For them is rising ground. Can they never tell
What is dragging them back, and how it will end?
    Not at night?

Old Fools' Time

Not when the strangers come? Never, throughout
The whole hideous inverted childhood? Well,
   We shall find out.

Philip Larkin

Well, 'we shall find out.' Only Larkin didn't. Cancer, that ravenous shark, took him first. I only hope that before the end, they turned him into an instant junkie. His muse may have deserted him some time before, his views are hard to take, but unnecessary pain, if avoidable, is indefensible. He was without what they used to call, and perhaps still do, 'the consolation of faith'.

    ... the bits that were you
    Start speeding away from each other for ever

As an almost life-long atheist myself, I find it reassuring to come across others, in this case whatever his shortcomings as a human being, as a prop to one's own non-faith. Better cancer – not much better but better nevertheless – than to become a smelly old mindless cabbage dribbling at one end and leaking at the other.

Another man, whom, in this case, I admire unreservedly, is the late Spanish film-maker Luis Buñuel. I've just re-read his autobiography *My Last Breath* (*Last Sigh* in ostrich-minded America) which, with the help of his friend and colleague Jean-Claude Carrière, he completed not long before his death in 1983. In it he made the following admirably sensible request: 'Some doctors do help us to die, but most are only money-makers who live by the canons of an impersonal technology. If they would only let us die when the moment comes and help us to go more easily. Respect for human life becomes absurd when it leads to insufferable suffering.'

Ever honest, early in that same last testament he admits that in his seventies (he made his last film in 1976) he enjoyed what he called 'playing at senility', but became, as his final decade passed by, 'increasingly conscious of my decrepitude' and 'only happy at home following my routine', the twin peaks of his day being two dry martinis, always his favourite tipple, one before lunch, the other before dinner, although he admits to sometimes cheating and drinking the latter before its designated hour. Later anyway he was forced to substitute the martinis with red wine.

In my late seventies I am still able to play at senility, enjoying supportive friends, singing, albeit seated and wearing an eye-patch, drinking Irish whiskey, fly-fishing for trout, looking at works of art and listening to Bessie Smith, the Empress of the Blues. I imagine this last will be the last to go.

I have, however, put the block on my tendency to flirt. This is partly from observing others of my generation failing to recognize how pathetic they look ogling young women, and confirmed by watching myself on a video tape rolling my eyes at a pretty chat-show hostess. On the other hand I still look forward to what I think of as 'treats', the equivalent of a child anticipating a visit to a circus or pantomime (my choices here date me like the rings on a tree stump).

I have realized recently that I share some defects with most of my generation. This very morning I rang up two old friends. One, a few years older than I, couldn't remember the title of a play he had seen quite recently (a general failing of mine also) and, as he struggled to find it in that jumbled

'I have, however, put the block on my tendency to flirt'

filing cabinet we oldies call our brains, I recognized his mounting irritation. I would bet also that some time later, and for no logical reason, it surfaced.

The Frankenstein compulsion in scientists, angrily recognized by Buñuel, was confirmed for me on Waterloo station only a few weeks ago. Returning from the country and on my way to a friend's sixtieth birthday party in NW1 (a treat), I went into a large stationer's to buy him a card to accompany a bottle of malt whisky in its protective and decorative drum. As is usual these days, there were many cards designed for special recipients: the newborn, or at any rate their parents, toddlers, 'cool' teenagers, engaged couples (The longest sentence in the English language? 'I do'), rose-cheeked grandparents on their retirement, but there wasn't, and I'd half expected it, a card aimed specifically at anyone of sixty, today an unremarkable age. There were, on the other hand, several, mostly smothered in rose-clad cottages in low relief, for centenarians!

To justify these cards economically implies a substantial number of potential recipients, and they've promised us that soon a hundred and fifty to two hundred will be the norm, but why? What for? What will be, to use a fashionable cliché, 'the quality' of the double centenarians' lives? One thing's for sure: the Queen, famous for turning off lights at Buckingham Palace and having torn sheets repaired, will surely stop sending telegrams, or their more expensive modern equivalents, to those who have survived a mere century.

I bought one of these cards for my friend and wrote underneath the Patience Strong-like verse, the famous and refreshingly cynical and accurate riddle:

Q: Who wants to live to be a hundred?
A: Someone of ninety-nine.

Of course there are some people who enjoy life well into old fools' territory. Like heavy smokers who can always cite an uncle who lived into his nineties on sixty full-strength Capstans a day, only to be eventually run over, when drunk, by a bus, most of us know or have known someone who kept all their marbles into their nineties, and enjoyed every day as it came.

In my case it was Eileen Agar, a witty and beautiful old painter who claimed to have one abstract leg and one surrealist, who had slept in the same bed (but not at the same time) as Picasso, who drank champagne every day, and whose funeral was conducted by a close friend who was a Catholic priest. As he knew that she was an atheist, there were no prayers or hymns. I bet he prayed for her in silence though.

In her autobiography, dictated like Buñuel's towards the end of her life, she expressed the hope that she would 'die at a sparkling moment', and so she did. Her happy end was rare though. Not to be relied on.

Indeed not! My mother, for example, died in her nineties, in Shakespeare's seventh age, *sans* teeth, *sans* eyes, *sans* taste, *sans* everything. My father had died aged sixty-one of a perforated ulcer. My mother and I were at his deathbed in a Liverpool hospital. The West Indian nurse knew exactly when he was going. I looked at his corpse, but his humorous lethargic spirit had left only a shell, an envelope. What surprised me, and later on my sister when she got there, was how calmly my mother took it. They'd been married for forty years, but she didn't weep and all she said to the nurse was (embarrassing, as she often was), 'My son has many coloured friends.' A week later she even went on a fishing trip with me to a hotel in North Lancashire that my father had booked for us both some weeks before. I found out later that this calm interlude is by no means uncommon. Some block (chemical? psychological? both?) would seem to protect the bereaved from reacting immediately to the death. Maud was even in total control at the funeral.

A few weeks later the dam burst, the river broke its banks. She cried much of the time and reproached herself continually for sometimes criticizing Tom (not without reason) for drinking too much, all this interwoven with endless reminiscing about their life together.

Gradually she recovered. My sister, brother and I persuaded her, without too much difficulty, to sell the big house in Liverpool where she'd lived for twenty-six years and move to Brighton (we all lived in the south by then), and Andrée found her a big flat with a lift, on the front overlooking the wrinkled sea and the still splendid pavilion pier.

Her life seemed worth living again. There were grandchildren, visits to the theatre, family Christmas at one or the other of us in rotation, while, in Brighton itself, she kept up with several retired theatricals, most of them elderly gays.

She only revisited Liverpool once and came back to Brighton saying that she didn't 'care for it any more', although, until she'd moved, she'd lived there all her life within a quarter of a mile. Too many ghosts, perhaps. Or, more likely, the fact that she was no longer at the centre of a mildly Bohemian circle, no longer the queen of queens?

Although eight years older than Tom she was to outlive him by over twenty years. She hadn't drunk anything beyond the occasional ginger-beer shandy on very hot days, or, even more rarely, a Tia Maria, for she had a very sweet tooth. As for smoking, only very occasionally in the loo, if she felt it politic to mask the pong. Even so, and inevitably, true old age was beginning to growl quietly in its corner and show its yellow teeth.

Faced with various small accidents of a potentially danger-ous nature, Andrée decided it was time to move Maud to somewhere where she could keep a closer eye on her and settled for a small flat in commuter-ridden Surrey. The flat was directly opposite a health-food store, somewhat ahead of its time, which Andrée and her husband, Oscar, had opened after their semi-retirement from the stage. This enabled Andrée to 'pop across the road', as Maud put it, to check she was all right. ('Pop' was a favourite word of my mother's. Before it drew closer, she always referred to her own death as 'popping off'.)

Andrée warned me after a time that Maud was beginning to lose her marbles, but I didn't really take this in until, on one of my rather infrequent visits, I realized she was talking disconnected nonsense. Without 'drawing breath', an expression she used to describe non-stop verbalizers, she told me that footballers shouldn't wear beards as it stopped them playing well (she had never shown the least interest in the game, but detested facial hair), that she couldn't under-stand why she was so obsessed with Barry Manilow (she had always favoured thin, camp men) and finally asked what did Billie Jean King and her partner 'do'. She had forgotten that during the forties she told me that she'd had several erotic dreams involving a very glamorous actress at the Liverpool Playhouse. I didn't remind her of this except to say that surely she didn't intend to come out in her late eighties? She would once have found this funny, but no longer. 'No, of course not!' she said, crossly.

There were several later eccentric conversations, by then confined to her family and a few visitors. Andrée and I, while realizing how sad it was, also became on occasion hysterical with laughter.

The most far-out demonstration of Maud's gradual loss of reality was when she asked Andrée's help to fill in a form. Knowing official forms can be difficult to fill in, Andrée asked to see it. It was an advertisement cut out, not too well, from the *Daily Mail*. 'JOIN THE RAF AND LEARN TO FLY' was the headline. Despite the fact that there was an age limit involved (18–25), Maud was convinced it was her duty. Her daughter reminded her that, apart from one childhood day-trip to the Isle of Man, she'd been too scared to go on a ship, let alone fly, and then there was the question of her age. So, finally, although it took some time, Maud relinquished her 'duty'.

The thought of the old lady, very shrunken and bent by this time, doing her preliminary training on the parade ground, or putting on her goggles and leather helmet as she ran towards her fighter, really set us off. I laughed as if I'd been smoking too much dope.

It was sad, harmless and comic, but quite soon her growing dementia spread outside. The Cranley newsagent complained she had started to ring him up at two or three in the morning to ask why the papers hadn't been delivered.

Not that she read them when they did arrive. At first she

used to tick off, and later encircle, every word, article by article, until the whole issue was obliterated. Then, a few months later, she began to scrumple all the pages into a ball and staple everything together to retain its shape. I asked Andrée if she thought an avant-garde gallery might be interested. Today it would have won the Turner Prize (Maud Melly's three periods: ticks, circles and scrumples).

It was Andrée who convinced her brothers, Bill and me, that it was essential Maudie went into a home. Andrée had already had a disturbing shock when, crossing the road from Nuts of Cranley to check on her, she found our mother apparently dead. Andrée's pocket mirror failed to cloud over and she could find no pulse, so she sat down to think about what to do next. Whom should she ring first? My brother and me? Maudie's doctor? An ambulance? Do you have to tell the police first? Suddenly the phone rang. Maudie reached for it and said, in a perfectly normal voice, 'Maud Melly, here.'

Andrée is a brilliant raconteuse, and when she told us this story it seemed very funny. But then, only a comparatively short time later, she yet again crossed the road and opened the door to find Maudie lying at the bottom of a steep staircase leading up to her flat. She was unconscious, her limbs splayed out like those 1920s Pierrot dolls you sometimes used to find flopped over the round pale green tasselled cushions on the rather grubby settees of ageing flappers.

This time it was to the hospital, with sprains, bruises and, I think, several broken ribs. When Maud returned to her flat Andrée had already contacted a suitable and sympathetic home. She had naturally become alarmed that her postmodernist parent might have another fall and break something, scald herself or set herself on fire. Moving an aged parent into a home is considered a very cruel thing to do – and sometimes it may well be – but in Maudie's case it was totally justified and besides she welcomed it. Having worked on the newspaper she had nothing to do before Andrée came over at lunchtime. In Liverpool she'd always read a great deal, mainly choice middle-brow novels with a pinch of what she called 'spice', but she couldn't concentrate any more. She did spend a lot of time watching television, but it was difficult to say how much she took in. Among her favourite programmes was snooker, although as she obstinately refused to have a colour set she can't have made much of it.

For her the old people's home, despite being called Allyblasters, a curiously aggressive name for a haven of rest, was a great improvement. She had a large room with a big picture window overlooking woods and fields and 'her own things round her', a condition for senile contentment supported by those who are not yet senile themselves. Who is to say?

The matron and staff were both helpful and attentive (it was after all a private nursing-home, although I recently visited a state institution in Hastings which, while less luxuriously appointed, seemed just as friendly). Maud had always gone out of her way to court popularity. She told me that at Allyblasters she was much the most popular inmate with the nurses. Perhaps she was, but I dare say her mixture of swanking (about us) and snobbery (about whom she'd known, preferably titled) must have tried their patience at times. Even so, once when I was leaving, one of the old ladies, as she invariably referred to her in some cases slightly younger contemporaries, ran out on to the landing and, leaning over the banisters, gave me a right earful of scatological and anatomical abuse. Having a great-aunt, a saintly figure for most of her long life who did the same towards the end of it, I was not too surprised, but in the hall matron apologized and told me that, of course, 'Mrs Melly would never do that.'

Her ninetieth birthday was quite a success, although I don't think she recognized many of those present. She certainly ate an enormous quantity of cake – apparently greed is a common trait among the very old – and seemed quite pleased to be the centre of attention even among people largely unknown to her.

From then on it was increasingly 'Old Fools' Time'.

My sister was with her when she died. Maud, she told me, looked at her intensely. She held on to her daughter's finger like a vice. She didn't let go until she let go. She seemed to remember nothing.

Maud was born into a world of cab-horses and died after people had walked on the moon. She'd 'come out', put her hair up and worn huge hats, cemeteries for dead birds, before the First World War. Admirers had written to her from the trenches. In the twenties she'd danced the Charleston, met and married my father, given birth to two boys and, unexpectedly, a daughter. She 'went up to London' once a year and 'did' several shows, mostly revues. She entertained a great deal and was a successful amateur actress. She sat out the Blitz and, although she always maintained her forties were her best decade, had quite a good time until Tom's death. All forgotten. Nothing in the end but Andrée's finger.

At her funeral in a Surrey crematorium, after we'd witnessed Maud's boxed disappearance between the blue velvet, multi-screen cinema curtains and emerged into 'the garden of remembrance', my brother Bill said to me, 'Death is a mysterious thing, isn't it?' It wasn't a startling observation, nor yet an eloquent image, but it's true enough.

2. A Prisoner on Remand

It's 6.35 on a January evening and I got up only about an hour ago. Increasingly I am becoming a sleepaholic, but this, coupled with wide-eyed insomnia between around 3 and 6 a.m., is temporary (at least I hope it's temporary). The explanation is that quite recently I was appearing at Ronnie Scott's Jazz Club and never in bed much before 4 a.m. (and then in a state of euphoric over-stimulation). I'm hoping my extended or disturbed sleep pattern is caused by this variation of jet-lag and not just old age. Since I got up I've eaten two bananas, swallowed a small Irish whiskey and watched an instalment of *The Simpsons*, my top-favourite programme.

It's dark outside in Shepherd's Bush and, it would seem, very cold. I've gathered this from my friend and lodger Desdemona, who comes from Zimbabwe. She has just got in from art school and put a freezing hand on my cheek. Her role here, in exchange for a rather small room and other advantages, is to make sure I'm on course, to sort my laundry and do some shopping if Diana's away or in the country. She's witty and chatty, although her high-pitched African accent and rapid delivery are sometimes difficult for me to understand. She's not unique there, however. I find almost everybody difficult to understand due to my escalating deafness.

I ask Desdemona to show me how to insert, play and eject a DVD. As the twenty-first century's Ned Ludd this took me some time to grasp and, as my memory is more and more like an old colander rusting away at the bottom of a polluted canal, I'll no doubt need a refresher course almost immediately. Finally I get to sit at my desk and get on with this book, a New Year's resolution after a long prevaricatory delay. At 1 a.m., after yet another banana and a glug of the Jameson, I climb wearily to bed. Was three bananas all I had to eat all day? Yes. Diana, who always cooks supper, was at the pictures with a friend and, although there is a small kitchen on this floor that I share with Desdemona, plenty of food in our fridge and a microwave I have finally mastered, I just couldn't be bothered. In general in the last few years my appetite has become much less demanding.

People who know nothing of my set-up will wonder who Diana is and of course she will appear from now on, frequently, in the text. I've been married to her for over forty years and more or less take it for granted that everyone is aware of our situation, especially as I've written about our meeting and subsequent life in earlier books. This volume I don't think would ever have been finished without her pressure. Our marriage began passionately and is finishing with compassion. She makes sure I do what I have to do, go where I'm meant to go, and I still love her very much.

10 January

Despite a sleeping pill, admittedly not a strong one, I woke at four and channel-jumped on my bedside television. On BBC 1 I found a riveting if repellent documentary on human parasites, giving pride of place to the tapeworm, a surprisingly recent discovery. It was partially dramatized, so I watched a rather unpleasant-looking Victorian hirsute doctor who, suspecting the existence of something of the sort, fed an egg to a condemned criminal six weeks before his execution. After this had been carried out, he was cut down, and an autopsy revealed the creature growing in his intestine. The doctor, explained the narrator, was much criticized for his methods.

A more cheerful episode showed a plump young man who volunteered for an experiment, a deliberate infestation, providing he was rid of it before his coming marriage. This was done, and he lay on the grass next to it. It was over six feet long, but he had lost several stone and was fitted for a most elegant wedding outfit he couldn't have done up earlier.

This confirmed a story I heard long ago of yet another Regency doctor, apothecary or quack, who became famous for helping young women to lose weight. He sold them tapeworm eggs as slimming pills and they were all, for a time, fully satisfied. I myself have recently lost several stone, but no one has suggested I have a tapeworm. I just eat less.

This unpleasant creature, while the star of the show, was not the only member of the cast. There was a very sympathetic young rock singer whose left eye had been eaten away by some tiny horrors picked up in the Far East, and an admirable young woman who had spent a lot of time in Africa treating infested and starving village children and adults. Via an insect bite she had developed elephantiasis, as yet only in one leg. We had a good look at that too, hideously enlarged, grey and heavily wrinkled. They are trying a new cure on her, but won't know if it works for several years. She was clearly of a sweet and courageous nature, but I couldn't help recalling the cynical aphorism, 'No good deed deserves to go unpunished.'

'*I am becoming a sleepaholic*'

It is remarkable, however, that by now we are able, through exposure by the box, to watch almost anything without fainting or vomiting: operations, the slaughter and dismemberment of animals, extreme brutality and, of course, birth. I remember a Jewish comedienne (Maureen Lipman perhaps) complaining that you couldn't turn on the TV any more without someone 'having a baby in your face'. I don't say it isn't better that we should be able to accept what we are all of us in part responsible for, but I sometimes suspect an element of gloating, like the way a crowd materializes instantly around a bad car crash.

Perhaps it's a constant in human nature. It wasn't so long ago after all that we stopped public hangings, banned dog-fights, cock-fighting and bear-baiting; and, in secret, some people are still digging out badgers to watch them torn to pieces.

William Blake, always appalled by human cruelty – one of the reasons they thought he was mad – in one of his many jousts with God, or Old Nobodaddy as he sometimes called Him, asked Him how, on the one hand, He could create the 'tyger' and, on the other, the lamb. It's even more puzzling why He should have invented the tapeworm. It's one of the many reasons I find it impossible to believe in the possibility of a beneficent 'personal' deity, let alone a judgemental one.

'Everything that is squint-eyed, doddering and grotesque is summed up for me in this one word, God.' *André Breton*

Of course I watched the tapeworms writhing, wriggling and growing ever longer until the last frame, and fell into a deep sleep which lasted until midday.

*

I now take a cornucopia of pills, some once a week, most daily. Recognizing my increasing tendency to make a muddle, Diana or sometimes Desdemona (surely an odd choice of name for an African?) fill up a plastic blue or violet pill-box divided vertically into the time of day and horizontally the days of the week. This box looks rather like a tiny chicken's battery system. The pills themselves are of many colours, sizes and shapes, like distorted Smarties. They are to fend off various threats. There are four tiny yellow ones, but only for Monday mornings. These are to suppress psoriasis, an unsightly disease in which an over-production of cells piles up on the surface of the skin and flakes off to leave patches of raw flesh (another example of God in a bad mood). I seem to have inherited this complaint from a great-uncle who developed it so badly that he never married because of the shock and repugnance it would cause his bride when, on their wedding night, he removed his combinations. As far as I know I was the only one among his nephews, nieces and a wide younger generation of cousins to inherit this grisly heirloom. In my case it did not surface until my early sixties, but from then on it never restrained itself. Happily it didn't attack my face, but the rest of me was covered with it. Naked, not by then a pretty sight at the best of times, I looked like a plant-eating dinosaur who had survived an unsuccessful attack by prehistoric raptors. Luckily the yellow pills defeated the disease, except for a small sprinkling on my knees and elbows. They are, however, apparently very powerful and can affect the liver and/or kidneys.

My first skin specialist, the good Dr Fry at St Mary's Paddington, demanded regular blood tests. I don't mind these, although I am not fond of the needle and give an involuntary squeak when one pricks my skin (my father tended to faint). Once I was quite amused by a nurse, evidently a black humorist, who had covered the walls of her small room with Dracula posters, and hung a realistic imitation bat from the ceiling. She, alas, has gone, taking her bat and posters with her.

Dr Fry, who treated me during the disease's heyday, never prescribed the yellow pills; perhaps they were not yet available. Instead he offered me a cream or ointment to rub on. It did no good except to alleviate the itching that led to inadvisable scratching (my bed at times resembled a butcher's shop in which someone had spilt several packets of cornflakes). He told me there *was* a certain cure: a month or so on the shores of the Dead Sea and frequent immersion in its waters, so saturated in natural minerals and salts that it's impossible to sink. (The Dead Sea provided the setting for one of my favourite pictures, Holman Hunt's *The Scapegoat*, which hangs in the Lady Lever Art Gallery in Port Sunlight, opposite Liverpool.) He added, however, that on one's return with skin like a baby's bottom, almost immediately the psoriasis would erupt again with equal vigour. In consequence I decided it wasn't worth it, and he agreed with me.

He did, however, propose I try another possible avenue of help, a twice-weekly visit to a department many floors up in another branch of the hospital. I warned him that, due to contracted singing engagements all over the British Isles and commissioned travel articles abroad, I might find it impossible to make every appointment. He said he quite understood.

What I had to undergo was exposure to ultra-violet light, brief at first, then building up gradually to around twenty minutes. He warned me that the nurse in charge had been there for many years, was in fact well past her official retiring age, but insisted on carrying on and was, he added with a twinkle in his eye for he was a drily humorous man, 'of the old school'. And so she was.

She was tiny, with spectacles, and wore a spotless white coat. She spoke with the educated yet brisk accent of the headmistress of a posh girls' school. Her shoes were white plimsoles. Her surgery was not especially large, but contained three separate cubicles side by side, the size and shape of police boxes and, to add to this comparison, the same dark blue. I always thought of the one I entered as Dr Who's Tardis. Each had a small rectangular window let in to the door so she could, from time to time, check you were all right. There was also an individual switchboard to turn on the strip-lights inside, and a timer to make sure you were not exposed for too long or short a period.

At the other end of the room was a short square box where patients could sit, like the assassinated Marat (who also had psoriasis), if only their lower bodies were affected. Along one wall, at right angles to the police boxes, was a row of small compartments where you stripped behind floral curtains with hooks to hang up your clothes. On my first visit Miss Day told me always to bring dark glasses to protect my eyes.

The door to the room was between the Tardis and the compartments. On the outside was a stern warning: 'Knock and wait!' If she was busy, the wait could take some time and, on my first visit, I presumed she hadn't heard and knocked again. When she did respond, she snapped, 'I always hear. You must be patient!' I never knocked twice again.

On my many appointments, travelling up in a rather old-fashioned lift usually in the company of others en route to time and space travel – it was somehow comforting that they were all fellow sufferers to a greater or lesser degree – I got to know and grew fond of Miss Day. On arrival, before undressing, you stood at her desk while she filled in your details: how long since your last visit, the length of time you were due to stand in the Tardis and so on, into a large leather-bound book like those in which you register in old-fashioned hotels. Her writing was, somehow predictably, both small and neat.

At first, although my specialist had written her a note of explanation, she took my non-appearances rather amiss, but then, after I'd spent a fortnight in Kenya, she read my commissioned article in the *Evening Standard* and from then on ('You write very well, Mr Melly') became much friendlier and, while far from indiscreet, did let drop one or two facts about her life.

She lived, she told me, in a flat in Victoria and knew many of the people who travelled on the 7.30 bus, but not to talk to. She had worked in the psoriasis department for thirteen years but had no intention of retiring, although she'd been entitled to seven years earlier. Her work, she implied, was her life. I gathered no idea of her political bias or taste in any of the arts. Had she friends or relatives? What was her background, her history? One thing she did make clear was her admiration, almost idolatry, of the specialist, Dr Fry. She gave me the impression that, on his rare visits, the Queen herself could not have been greeted with more reverence.

On her windowsill was an unexpected object, a small wireless set continuously tuned to Radio One, but very quietly. It stood next to the only other non-functional item in the room, a modest pot plant with very small, rather waxy red flowers. Was it hers? A present from a grateful patient? The former I doubt, the latter also. In my experience no one ever seemed to be cured; nor was her manner one to encourage a spontaneous gift. A mystery then.

She was not after all one to curb her tongue. I remember once a middle-aged man, old-style working class and not in the least aggressive, emerged from his cubicle as she passed by. She asked him tartly, 'And when did you last have a bath?' While she had a point, her question seemed to me both cruel and unnecessary.

Only once did I see her meet her match. A street-cred girl wearing tight jeans, T-shirt, leather jacket and clumpy shoes appeared quite late for her appointment and Miss Day predictably told her off. The girl looked at her with cool indifference and, in a strong Estuary accent peppered with numerous glottals and with every sentence ending with a question, explained that that morning (and I suspect many others) she hadn't the fare for the bus, had been sussed and thrown off and had to walk the rest of the way, 'Din't I?' Miss Day redirected her attack, telling her it was very wrong to get on the bus at all without her fare. The girl shrugged as though addressed by a lunatic and went into her cubicle to undress.

I thought Miss Day would be furious, but when she walked past me, I was surprised to see a suppressed smile.

She said, almost roguishly, 'You can't help laughing, can you?'

I quite enjoyed my appointments but not the treatment. It wasn't too bad to start with, when five minutes was my limit, but, after many weeks, when half an hour was my lot, it became excruciatingly boring. Inside, 'the Tardis' was no time-ship but just a small space. You stood on a duckboard with your own paper mat over it, surrounded by the tubes of ultra-violet lights. It was impossible to read in your special dark glasses (she tested them to see they were adequate) and the only diversion was the occasional glimpse of Miss Day looking through the observation glass like a conscientious prison wardress.

I tried various ways to reduce the tedium: dreaming of hooking trout, coming across Van Gogh on a visit to Arles and buying his entire production, but none of them really worked for long. When your bell rang and she let you out it was indeed like being released from prison.

Nor did I get any better. The unsightly complaint swung slightly between frightful and marginally less frightful, but only one person thought it was an advantage. That was my step-granddaughter, Katie, aged five or so. We were in Kenya and visiting the Muthaga Club – at the centre of the largely aristocratic 'Happy Valley' set famed for debauchery and drunkenness during the last war, which had been rocked by the murder of one of its members, Joss Erroll. With us was Petal Allen who, as a child in the forties, had known many of those concerned.

Much later this unsolved Agatha Christie-like mystery fascinated Cyril Connolly who began to investigate it with the writer James Fox. The Muthaga Club, airy and luxuriously sparse, remains largely as Fox described it in his fascinating book *White Mischief*, but, with the independence of Kenya, now has naturally enough a mixed membership.

Diana and I had with us Katie (later renamed Kezzie at her insistence). She was outside at the pool talking to a small group of black children. We crossed the lawn, Diana carrying a plate with chicken on it in case Katie/Kezzie was hungry, when a large kite swooped down and, seizing it in its claws, zoomed off again. Recovering from this shock we walked on and, as we approached the pool, I heard my step-grandchild boasting to her indifferent African audience, 'My grandfather is *quite* famous, and has psoriasis.'

I didn't include this in the article Miss Day admired, but I told her on my return and she was quite tickled.

Now and then Dr Fry would see me. He admitted I had hardly, if indeed at all, improved. I asked him if there was a possible cure (the Dead Sea the exception) and he said no; the trouble being, he explained with mildly cynical resignation, that psoriasis was not a killer, just a burden.

Eventually Miss Day began to lose her grip. The time I spent in the Tardis varied wildly from a few minutes to longer than the statutory half hour. She started to forget our names. Her time was surely drawing to a close. Dr Fry got to know this. I didn't tell him, I was too fond of her to sneak, but somebody did. He had recently acquired an assistant, a gentle and charming Asian girl, and he sent her down to 'help' Miss Day. Miss Day was the opposite of co-operative, let alone grateful, and the girl might as well not have been there. She was not allowed to touch the time switches or address the patients. I suspect, perhaps correctly, that Miss Day saw her as a spy.

One day, after a gap when I revisited Kenya for another newspaper, I came up in the lift to find Miss Day, her plant and radio, gone. Shortly afterwards Dr Fry told me he had *insisted*, and I don't suppose it was an easy confrontation, that her time was up.

Later, Dr Fry announced that in recognition of long and in recent years voluntary service, they were going to give her a champagne party and a new television set. She had indeed told me some time before that her set was very old and she suspected it might be dangerous. In consequence she never switched it on, but now and then, when passing, would pat it as though it were a dog. They gave her a catalogue and Dr Fry said, with mild irritation, she had chosen the most expensive. I felt, but didn't say, that she was justified in doing this.

I was very touched to be asked (I half hoped at Miss Day's request) to her final thrash. It was to be held in a large and fairly new hotel in Marylebone Road shortly after the termination of the West Way and opposite the Western Eye Hospital, a branch of, although separate from, St Mary's Paddington, and which is later to play an important role in this story. The hotel, its exterior quite impressive in the late-Victorian/Edwardian manner, was, I understood, built as the Railways Union's headquarters. Inside it was even more imposing, with huge corridors, an impressive staircase, and a vast lounge with no ceiling but an open prospect right up to the glass dome.

I was not too surprised to be told that it had been a union building because I had visited another branch in Crewe which, while smaller, was equally grand, with elaborately carved wood and stained-glass windows in the Burne Jones tradition. This conspicious spending is quite explicable, not solely because at the time they were built the railwaymen were considered the aristocrats of the union movement, but also as a case of keeping up with the bosses. This helps explain too why African chiefs, however poor their subjects, are always driven about in huge and expensive cars. There are alas few Gandhis in this world.

There we all gathered, Dr Fry, his wife, various other medicos and of course Miss Day herself. The corks popped, speeches were made, canapés eaten. The very expensive TV wasn't handed over then because it had already been delivered to the flat in Victoria. Miss Day responded to the speeches and was both brief (always a blessing) and totally without emotion. I felt that even Dr Fry had been proved, by dismissing her, to have feet of clay. She gave the impression that, champagne or no champagne, TV or no TV, she'd much sooner be up in her eyrie asking people when they last had a bath. It was a slightly downbeat affair all round.

Quite soon Dr Fry himself retired and a Dr Powles, a very friendly woman, replaced him.

Not long after that I was crossing Praed Street following a check-up in one department or another en route to a pub, the Fountain Abbey, which conveniently faces the main gates of the hospital, when a cheerful man stopped me. He told me he'd seen me in the psoriasis room in the past. Did I know, there was now a pill which had completely cleared his up? I said I didn't, but would mention it on my next visit. Dr Powles admitted there was such a pill but was reluctant to prescribe it, as it was very strong and could have serious side effects affecting both the kidneys and the liver.

I told her I was fully prepared to put myself at risk. She said all right – on my own liver and kidneys be it. Dr Powles laid down a condition before prescribing the little yellow pills – frequent blood tests. It's a tiny price to pay as the skin disease disappeared as if by magic. To date my kidneys and liver are unaffected, although my own doctor, who knows I drink and have drunk all my life, is quite perplexed as to the latter. She says I'm a medical freak.

This chapter is the last for the moment to centre on St Mary's Hospital. Only for the moment, though. At my age I am like a prisoner on remand.

As a coda, here is the list of the various doctors and surgeons who prod and poke at me at longer or shorter intervals for various possible or proven physical weaknesses. What's odd though is that most of the time I feel pretty well, even optimistic.

There's no need to study this list in detail. It's just to prove I'm not malingering.

Dr Soucer – hearing
Prof. Johnston – endocrinology
Dr Kohn/Elkin – chest and allergy clinic
Dr Mitchell – ditto
Prof. Peters – cardiology
Dr Robinson – hepatology
Prof. Wickramesinghe (Wicks) – haematology.

3. A Fair Cop

'We'll overlook it this time, sir,' said a young policeman with that unique accent a friend of mine has identified as that (although not uniquely so) of Hendon Police College.

I had to admit that it had been 'a fair cop' ('archaic', surely). I'd been caught pissing up against a wall in a fairly dark alley off the Uxbridge Road, Shepherd's Bush. Knowing I had a card up my sleeve, I was prepared to admit all, including the awareness that I could be charged and fined.

And here I'll freeze the frame just as the young policeman asks me, 'And what are we doing here, sir?' his torch-beam catching the stream of golden urine which surely made his question superfluous.

'All is not gold that glisters,' said the monkey as he pissed in the sun.

But why stop the film at this point? Well, it's not simply to create tension, a sometimes effective device, especially in the cinema, but to own up to a distressing tendency of us old and ageing: a belief that one's youth was golden, a way to impress anyone under forty. Scornful of this when young oneself, now it's our turn to bore our younger friends' children. 'A night out in the West End including Marie Lloyd cost a halfpenny less than half-a-crown.' Fade and replace the old Edwardian barrow-boy with me (same pub, same stool). 'You may not believe this but in the fifties you could have half a dozen oysters in Wheelers, a grilled sole,

cheese and a bottle of house wine for around five pounds.'
Some of my young listeners express, as we did, polite incred-
ulity, masking the acquisition, I suspect, of useful material
for future mockery.

The old can be very touching. On television, veterans of
the First World War, and the occasional insertion of a faded
snapshot of them in uniform at eighteen, can bring a tear
to the most cynical eye, but an endless general banging on
about past financial advantages (the comparative increase in
average wages is seldom brought up) is to be avoided. I
pledge here to try to stick to the format under discussion or
that, if I find myself wandering off down a side path, this
must be fully justified by the relevance of the incident or
anecdote. Me and whose army?

On a TV programme the other night we assorted ageing
talking heads were meant to reveal what we would have
done differently if we'd known at twenty what we know
now. It was heavily edited but not unfascinating. Mo
Mowlam spoke a lot of good sense, but for me the star of
the show was Tony Benn. He came across as consistently
honest, even though his views are nationally unpopular, and
what's more he strongly advised us, his contemporaries, not
to rub the noses of the young in our 'glorious past' –
Aldermaston and all that. An admirable piece of counsel.

Joan Rivers was perhaps, on this showing, the antithesis
of the ex-pipe-smoking, ex-titled aristocrat. She spoke up in
favour of extreme 'vanity surgery' without qualification, and
in her case with considerable justification.

'She's had so many face-lifts, she has to cross her legs to
smile.' *Old joke*

But her view, insofar as I could judge, was that maintaining youth under the knife attracted money. It would seem to have worked in her case, and she and her rich plain husband fell in love and were happy until he died. As someone pointed out, it's unfair that men tend to become more attractive in middle age; lines and wrinkles seem to have an aphrodisiac effect. With women it's the reverse.

There was another American some time back for whom, whatever *she* might think, it had been a disaster. I have forgotten why she was for a short period so often on television or in the papers, perhaps an acrimonious divorce, but she looked like the Bride of Frankenstein in a wind tunnel. The trouble is we love disasters as long as they don't happen to us. In Terry Gilliam's brilliant nightmare *Brazil*, there are two women, devotees of plastic surgery. For one it succeeds: she becomes younger and younger throughout the movie. The other, on the contrary, increasingly turns into a wheelchaired freak. There is a German word, *schadenfreude*, meaning enjoyment of other people's mishaps and tragedies but Auden, as so often, found the perfect metaphor:

> That we are always glad
> When the Ugly Princess, parting the bushes, to find out why
>   the woodcutter's children are happy
> Disturbs a hornet's nest . . .

Joan Bakewell in the 'What would you have done differently?' programme was a paragon of tolerance: have a face-lift if it makes you feel better (Bakewell hadn't, and looked much the most beautiful on the screen); sow your wild oats when young; have fun etc. She is a true libertarian and stresses that it's *we* who must decide what we do. Like Terry Gilliam she is against all forms of thought-control, nanny-like rules, fascism in a word, from the imposition of 'no smoking' in restaurants, trains and soon bars (and I don't think she even smokes) to the emergence of a leader with a little moustache and a cow's-lick of hair. Good old Joan! You are still this ageing, impotent man's crumpet!

The difficulty of writing about the present is that everything is in flux: one's feelings, physical degeneration, memory, names, what, being deaf, one has taken in, or even, if one has, remembered. Writing about the past, as I have in the past, is a doddle in comparison because it's done, it's set, it's in three dimensions, the dead walk and talk there. So much was possible, each day might bring a revelation.

Now I sometimes feel like tiny Alice and the animals swimming in her own gargantuan tears. If I also feel like a motherless child, it's because I am!

Well now, I know you've all been straining at the leash to hear the conclusion of my confrontation with the policeman in the Uxbridge Road, W12 – or perhaps not. But still, here it is.

'If yer wants ter know the time ask a pliceman.' *Old music-hall song suggesting the law nicked the watches from unconscious drunks*

I explained to the law that every night I have to take a round white pill in order to expel the excess water from my system and this resulted in six to eight visits to the loo or the use of a hospital bottle if, in a hotel or guest-house, there was no bathroom en suite.

'*I sometimes feel like tiny Alice and the animals swimming in her own gargantuan tears*'

'You take this pill at night, sir?' the policeman checked, glancing at the same time at his watch. It was about twenty past ten. I admitted I hadn't taken it yet, but — I suggested he could check with his station's saw-bones — it could act retrospectively at any time, as I believed sometimes happens with an LSD backflash.

He wasn't prepared to give up yet, though. 'Where have you come from?'

'A Greek restaurant on the other side of the Uxbridge Road.'

'How far is it?'

'Past the church and two blocks along. It's called the Vine Leaves.'

'And why didn't you make use of the toilet facilities provided by that establishment?'

'I didn't want to at that time. The pill's demands are instantaneous. You have about ten seconds at most between the pressing need and its fulfilment; unless of course you prefer to wet yourself.'

He stood in thought for some time, a silhouette against the street lamps behind him. Then he passed judgement. 'Well, sir, this time we'll overlook it, but next time try not to choose the wall of a police station.'

4. The Oldest Living Surrealist in the World

...and can't remember who called this morning...
Philip Larkin

He looked at us from his hospital bed, mouth gaping, eyes open so wide as to indicate both bewilderment and mild panic. From time to time he would emit a sound that was almost a word. Before his stroke he'd known us both very well. I'd always thought then that he resembled a small lizard, full of compact energy, liable at any moment to run rapidly up the wall and across the ceiling. No lizard now.

In the pub across the road we discussed this metamorphosis. My friend Michael suggested that he was more like the unfortunate mouse turned up by Robert Burns's plough ('sleekit' and 'timorous' certainly). This comparison seemed to me all the more accurate because of his very large ears. He'd always had them, I suppose, although it is when they grow older that some people's suddenly do a Dumbo, and I'd never noticed his before. Now they seemed not only large but permanently cocked, like a small animal listening nervously for the pad or slither of a predator.

Unrecognized by him, I was glad that his daughter was at his bedside and that her small affectionate attentions (mopping his forehead, holding his hand) seemed to calm him at any rate for a time. I was pleased, not only because of this but also that she would presumably tell Ms Mogg that

Michael and I had come here on this baking day to visit him. She it was who had written to say that he had had a stroke, given me the address and asked me to go and see him, so here we were.

I've always liked and admired Ms Mogg, collector of horror films and the quiet but determined companion of our friend's later years. Early on in their relationship, given her slightly androgynous and somehow nautical air, I'd named her 'the Cabin Boy'. I felt now, after so long, loyal and devoted service, she should be promoted to Commander's Runner at least.

He was not in a single room. In the other bed was a stout old gentleman in a white gown. He wore a small black skull-cap, so I presumed he was Jewish. I whispered to Michael how closely he resembled the Pope. As we were leaving, some nurses were getting him out of bed and leading him gently but firmly out of the room. By the terrible smell he had obviously shat himself. Extreme old age seems to enjoy demeaning us, destroying what dignity we once had.

The confused old person in the hospital across the road was Conroy Maddox, so far as I know the oldest living surrealist in the world. Although already in his nineties, until his stroke he had continued to paint, make collages and create objects.

Since his refusal to participate in the great 1936 Exhibition on the grounds that too many of the British contributions were not surrealist at all (he had been quite right in this), he had stuck to his guns through the war, and afterwards through the dismissal of the movement as 'old hat', until its return to favour in the late sixties and seventies. He had even begun to sell well and been able to give up his day job, as semi-pro musicians call it (he was, so far as I know, a highly skilled technical draftsman), and paint full time.

I don't intend here to go further into his life or his art, as there are recent books covering both these subjects, but I would point out that lately there have been several major exhibitions and retrospectives in both London and the provinces and a celebratory lunch at the Tate Britain to honour his ninetieth birthday. He often appeared at private views, not only his own but others relevant to his interests. Afterwards, if there were a supper in a restaurant, he would stay late, drinking lots of wine and his favourite liqueurs with their alchemical colours. He would talk too, admittedly, in his later days, somewhat repetitively. His favourite 'surreal tale' was of Queen Victoria, puzzled as to what to give her grandson, Prince Wilhelm, later the Kaiser, for his twenty-first birthday. After much pondering she reached a solution. 'I know,' she said, 'I'll give him Kilimanjaro.' After a time I really began to enjoy the inevitable repetition of this anecdote, and Conroy with his black hair, heavy spectacles, small moustache and curious, almost lemon, complexion, was an age-defying lesson to us all, repetitive or not.

In recent years I had at his request opened several of his exhibitions including one in Ledbury, a rather interesting old town in the Midlands which was his birthplace. I mentioned it now to see if it struck a chord. 'You remember,' said his daughter, 'I drove you there from London.' Not a flicker of recognition or memory altered his vacant, seemingly empty bewilderment.

After about ten minutes Michael suggested to his daughter that we were tiring him. She thanked us for coming and we left, passing the incontinent Pope.

*

Michael Woods is a brilliant photographer, considerably younger than I but equally plagued by various physical ailments. A mutual friend sent him to see me, almost forty years ago now, to show me his images of the Portobello Road, not the 'me old cock sparrer' aspects of it, as I might have expected, but its melancholy boarded-up shops and people mumbling to themselves. He'd also taken portraits of many writers and painters, never obvious publicity shots but attempts to get behind the mask, and usually very successful.

I admired the work and recognized a surrealist eye. I was thinking of writing a book about Paris and suggested he became involved. As he knew very little about the movement I lent him several key books. Off he went via the Channel tunnel, to return with a portfolio beyond all my hopes. Furthermore he had not only photographed what Breton called 'elected places' (I had also given him a list of those aspects of the city the surrealists revered) but had recorded much else that seemed to him, and was, entirely relevant. The book was done, published and became a considerable and long-lived success.

We remained friends. He'd got to know Conroy and to photograph him often and with impressive understanding of his character, its virtues and failings, and so it was that we set out together to see the Wizard of Lambolle Road, NW3.

I have a terrible addiction to taxis, an extremely expensive addiction these days. The doctors tell me I should walk a little each day and, with every encouragement from Diana on economic as well as physical grounds, I do try, although I especially hate steps and stairs and having to change platforms; but on this expedition and accompanied by Michael Woods (whose Eeyore-like gloom alternates with sudden ill-suppressed bursts of laughter, an enjoyable contrast, or at least I find it so), I had resolved to hail cabs only in dire necessity.

And so we set off at midday, Michael tall and gaunt, me short and plump, like Don Quixote and Sancho Panza, on the hottest day of the year. Knowing a certain amount of walking and the ascent and descent of several flights of steps in tube stations would be involved, I took my stout but pretty stick with the doggie's-head handle.

The tube part didn't take too long, nor the change on to the Northern Line, nor our getting off at some obscure station I'd never heard of near Cricklewood, but there were three lots of steep stairs and I was glad of my stick. Thump thump it went, like that of Blind Pugh's in the first chapter of *Treasure Island*, but with less sinister intimations.

Emerging into a baking, anonymous suburb, we were immediately misdirected to the nearest taxi rank. Eventually we found the real one but only by retracing our steps and heading left instead of right. My ankles were beginning to give me gyp. I don't think I've ever enjoyed climbing into a taxi more.

Finally we arrived at the nursing home, a large Edwardian building with a curved forecourt. We went in, to be confronted by a very old, small, cross man in a dressing-gown whom a large African nurse took resignedly back to his room. Three minutes later he'd reappeared, making incomprehensible demands in an aggrieved treble whine.

The nice blonde receptionist told us that Conroy had been moved only two days previously to a hospital in

Hampstead, an institution much closer to my house in Shepherd's Bush.

I have a card that conjures up taxis, ordinary London cabs, which charge the fare to an account. I got the nice receptionist to ring for one and was told it would be twenty minutes. It took an hour to materialize ('terrible traffic, guv'). While we were waiting I sat on a narrow wall across the wide and busy road. Eventually Michael came across to me with the welcome news that the increasingly nice receptionist had asked us if we wouldn't prefer to sit in the garden, and she'd let us know when the cab finally arrived.

So we did, and it was like a senile version of Alice's mad tea party. At various tables under umbrellas sat the inmates. One old woman seated by herself gobbled up a huge load of Smarties with the urgency of an animal who fears that at any moment a stronger creature could emerge from the shrubbery to drive it off and gobble them up itself. Yet the most bizarre aspect of this garden of twitchers, cursers and blank-eyed phantoms was a small party of several inmates, one of whom was wearing one of those 'novelty hats', a towering green topper made, I believe, from felt. 'Well,' as Larkin wrote, 'we shall find out', but in my case, I hope not! Surely all the whiskey I've drunk, all the cigarettes I've smoked, will hopefully carry me off before, unlike my hero Falstaff, I grow 'as cold as any stone' and (to misquote) 'a babble of green top hats'.

It wasn't too far in the taxi and we quite quickly found Conroy on the fifth floor. After we left I was dying for an enormous gin and tonic. Michael's antibiotics forbade drink so he had a bottle of still water on one of those awkward, benched, wooden tables. Then we asked the way to a rank

(I'd given up my resolution to stick to public transport, free as it may be for OAPs), and were told there was one at the bottom of the long, steep hill with its fine Georgian houses. We paused so I could do one of my ten-seconds-or-else wees into a privet hedge, this time unconnected to the constabulary. No pedestrians passed on our side of the road but several cars did and probably saw what I was up to, but registered no critical disapproval or even surprise. Long ago, when I often did the same thing from being very drunk rather than from the need to get rid of excess water in the system with the aid of a nightly pill, I noticed that, wherever I was (Berkeley Square, for instance, on one bright afternoon), people just pretended I was invisible, a phantom pisser!

We, I mean the English, have this ability to imitate the three wise monkeys. On the tube, not so long ago but before my right hand developed taxi-itis, the carriage was full of businessmen, and women who'd been shopping, when the door between the coaches opened and five youths burst in. 'You're a load of fuckin' wankers!' they yelled at us. None of the passengers, including me, seemed to hear. One man turned over a page of his *Evening Standard*. The lads had another crack at it: 'A load of fuckin' wankers!' they repeated even more aggressively. No reaction. I imagined they'd fared no better in the previous carriages – or would in the next ones either. Nothing was said after their departure and I thought, 'I suppose that's what we are really – a load of fucking wankers – whether faced by a small body of yobs insulting homeward-bound commuters or the sight of a drunk jazz-singer urinating in Berkeley Square.' I suppose I personally had a feeble excuse – I might be thought of as too old to engage in fisticuffs.

At the bottom of the quite steep, quite long hill was a small circle of benches. Just beyond there was a busy main road with two more side streets a few yards to the right. Leaving me seated, Michael went on patrol there to see if he could intercept a cab plying for hire. In the next half hour only one passed and that occupied. I sat on.

I was not alone. On the other benches were about ten people swigging tins of strong lager and, to one degree or another, clearly pissed. They were not, however, the usual smelly old tramps who are regulars at most alfresco public houses, but rather young (middle twenties?) and fairly well dressed in that style which apes poverty—torn jeans, etc. – but gives itself away by being reasonably clean. They kissed a lot, and now and then one or two of them would begin to wander unsteadily off, only to return after a few yards to add another point to the repetitive and seemingly aimless conversation they'd been part of. At one stage a young woman staggered over to ask me if I had a light for her roll-up. When I said I hadn't, she smiled without rancour and returned unsteadily to her companions.

Finally Michael gave up and, more discontented than ever, said there was a rank at the top of the hill we'd recently descended and so of necessity we reascended it. By this time the 'short daily walk' advised by my doctors had become a long one. Thump, thump, thump, went my dog-headed stick, only by now my ankles had really begun to ache, my calves to stiffen and itch, and my mood grown closer to Blind Pugh, although with unfocused malice and no murderous intentions.

Thump, thump – we passed the great stranded whale of the hospital where the sad husk of Conroy gaped in his bed,

43

past the pub, onwards and upwards, until finally, at a church, we turned left and there (for a moment I thought it might be a mirage already booked to carry some wedding guests to their breakfast) there was a substantial row of cabs, most of them black but some painted in bright colours to advertise insurance or supermarkets. So we took the one at the front and asked it to stop near Notting Hill, where Michael lives, and then on a mile to Shepherd's Bush, where I do.

I ached all over but leant back in a state of relaxed bliss – like banging your head on a brick wall and then stopping.

I got home just before six, almost seven hours after we'd left and with seven minutes of it spent at Conroy's bedside. I slept until supper at eight, lurched upstairs again and, having swallowed my three night pills, one the water pill (six visits to the loo before 7 a.m.), fell into welcome oblivion.

5. One Last Disadvantage

Eyes, nose, mouth and chin,
That's the way to Uncle Jim.
Uncle Jim makes lemonade,
Round the corner chocolate's made.
Put a penny in the slot,
And out it comes, plop, plop, plop.
                              Schoolboys' jingle

It's now late November. In the interim I've been X-rayed, or scanned as they call it, moving very slowly on my back through a tube with the occasional flash of the camera above me. Not being claustrophobic, I didn't mind this, although as usual I squeaked when I was injected to 'relax the intestines', but positively enjoyed the psychedelic colours that flashed now and then down narrow bands along the sides of the tube.

I didn't however relish the small nozzle they had inserted into my arsehole. It was attached to a tube, itself connected to an air pump which then blew air up my intestines and into my stomach. Despite having been gay and then bisexual well into my twenties, I never took to anal penetration. At school, on the back stage of the puppet theatre he used for trysts on the art master's and mistress's day off as he had a key, a bigger boy, in every sense of the word, tried it and I fainted. During the fifties, when I had caught a dose of

45

clap, a nice Scottish doctor, the image of my favourite housemaster as it happened, wanted to examine my sperm. He put on a rubber glove, well greased, and inserted a finger. I fainted again. He told me when I came to that by the manipulation of some gland he'd got what he wanted. He added, as I dressed, that I was clearly the active rather than the passive partner.

They didn't find anything they now call 'threatening' in my examination. A few nodules and a small fissure was the best they could do, but even so they have decided to repeat the exercise, this time with an enema, in the near future. I've only had one enema in the past and didn't like it either. It was after I'd had a burst ulcer in the sixties. A large cheerful West Indian nurse was in charge of the operation. She was always asking me, even at this point, when my 'bit of spare' was coming to see me.

Some people, presumably passive gays, like enemas, and will even pay for the privilege of having one. Indeed there was a nurse who advertised her services in the personal column of a national newspaper. She's no longer there. I imagine they suspected her of canvassing non-medical cases, of attracting a non-prescribed clientele.

On this occasion, the scan discovered a nodule at the bottom of my lung. This was my second nodule; the other, higher up my lung, had vanished previously of its own volition. This new growth, however, very much interested my consultant, the totally admirable Dr Kohn, the ideal medico in my view. Of maybe Chinese or certainly Asian origin, and speaking perfect English without that harsh rapidity which so often accompanies Far Eastern origin, he explained again in full the possibilities of this phenomenon and then asked me what I wanted to do about it – a probe, chemical treatment or an immediate operation if the surgeon was prepared to do it, given my irregular heartbeat and other physical deterrents. Dr Kohn and his assistant, a nice woman, equally frank and in touch with Diana, told us that this last would, if it *were* cancer and I had a successful operation, put me professionally out of commission for at least, the very least, five or six weeks. It so happens that December and January I was meant to be very busy singing and, if I had to cancel my full date-sheet, it would not only harm my band-lead Digby Fairweather and his musicians but would prove a form of professional suicide. Bookers would be reluctant to renew their offers on the grounds that I could fall ill again.

Diana said I mustn't be influenced by money. We hadn't all that much as such, but two houses and lots of pictures, books and objects of, or so I believe, some concrete value. She would hate me to feel I might be not poor exactly, but broke. She wants me now to do anything I choose and, within my physical limitations, to enjoy myself. This time round too, she seemed less upset. During my first alarm she had asked several of her circle of friends, including my beloved sister, about my desire to have no treatment and they all without exception agreed I had made the right decision. Yet again, I said, 'No, no treatment, no tests, no medication, nothing!'

Dr Kohn said all right. He told us many patients in my position were prepared to try any possibility of a cure, no matter how painful or possibly unsuccessful, but others, like myself, were not. Of course I've taken into account I am in my late seventies. At under, say, sixty, I'd possibly have been less adamant – but more likely not either. Above all I want to avoid becoming an old fool, like several very senior citizens of my acquaintance (what a load of verbal under-the-carpet-sweepers we have become). I've seen too many 'senior citizens', Conroy Maddox for a recent example.

Selfish? What of those who'll miss me? Well, they'll do that, I suppose, whatever I die of. In my experience, however, they'll get over it. Affection eventually replaces grief. Anecdotes, usually humorous rather than adulatory, supplant tears or are proof of diminishing loss. One's moment of death is not in one's hands anyway. It's fate which kills you.

'He rambled and he gambled and the butcher had to cut him down.' *Old New Orleans funeral chant*

I also have incipient emphysema, a killer with no cure, which prevents breathing. As it progresses, oxygen helps, but finally there's nothing. You drown in your own water-logged lungs. I've read a certain amount about it: the late and remarkable Ken Tynan crawling about the floor battling for breath; a friend of Digby's, who, he told me very reluct-antly only when I pressed him, on his final visit was projectile-vomiting blood at the walls of his hospital room. So I've two horses galloping towards Death's losing post. I'd prefer cancer as at least they drug you with morphine, and to die a happy junkie is surely preferable to redecorating a hospital ward.

The good Dr Kohn, after the reappearance of this second white nodule, had the entire lungs re-scanned. He told me that if I continued to smoke, the emphysema was certain to accelerate. I do smoke. My struggle (not very heartfelt) against it, despite the support of Diana, has failed several

48

times, but that is a fairly recent issue. I'll bet then, I hope, on a cancer pipping the post.

Aside from degenerating hearing, weaker eyesight, occasional difficulty with stairs unless they have a banister, feeling faint if I get up too fast from a chair or bed and other minor difficulties, I'm not, they tell me with some surprise, in bad nick. There is, however, one last disadvantage, and not for those with a refined sensibility. For several years before my general physical degeneration I have been occasionally caught by an unexpected attack of violent diarrhoea. Among other places this happened twice in Liverpool, my home town, in a very primitive public toilet on Exchange Street East station and, as was so often the case, I was just too late, and another time when staying at my dear Uncle Alan's flat, but, worst of all, in the Victoria and Albert Museum. I'd gone there after lunch with a friend but, once inside the front entrance, I knew the curse had come upon me. On asking, I discovered the gents was at the other end of the building, past about forty collections of Ming china and other exhibits. It was impossible (I was now desperate) to even contemplate trying to make it, so I dived, jumping from foot to foot and clenching my bottom, into the ladies. Too late even so, but luckily there was plenty of paper to clean up both me and the cubicle. I didn't dare use the wash-basin, however, for fear of encountering a stern woman academic here to study Meissen hard porcelain, and taken short.

I always try to cover my tracks as far as I can, but a full shower and change of clothing are hardly ever immediately available. After one disaster in Digby Fairweather's partner's car, I now, on Diana's insistence, pay whichever member of the band is driving me 'danger money' and sit on a blanket or old towel.

I have elsewhere (in *Hooked*, my fishing memoir) talked of the unsought laxative effect of wearing breast-waders. I have checked with other elderly fishermen and found much confirmation. This, too, explains why my father always pocketed a substantial wad of loo paper before going down to the river. I've taken, therefore, to wearing grown-up nappies held in place not by a pin or adhesive band but by a pair of strong but gossamer-like underpants. Since I've had them, and I put them on now every day even when not fishing, there's not been a trace of the trots – naturally! This could, however, be due to the wisdom of Dr Watson, who not only prescribed them, but after listening to my symptoms said it sounded like constipation. 'Surely the reverse!' I cried in disbelief. She explained that, on the contrary, water, which I have to drink in great quantities to replace the amount pissed away each disturbed night by my anti-water-retaining pills, seeps into the blockage of constipated matter and breaks it up into a loose but irresistible force, in which case it's back to the V & A ladies or its equivalent. Now, if I miss a day, I swallow a mild laxative, a pink powder whisked round in a glass until it dissolves, and perfectly pleasant-tasting too, and it would seem (touch the wood of the loo) to prevent this disaster recurring. There are certain foods which seemed to sabotage my intestines in my pre-nappy days. They are bacon and potted Morecambe Bay shrimps, on both of which I dote but still mistrust, and, like citrus fruit, tomatoes, strawberries and wine, which give me arthritis, I still avoid.

*

'I have elsewhere . . . talked of the unsought laxative effect of wearing breast-waders'

For several days recently I've been staying with one of my oldest and closest near contemporaries, Andy Garnett, who makes later and fuller appearances in our shared dotage. During the night there I've been woken many times over four hours by my anti-water-retention pills – the loo is just across the corridor in the very comfortable converted out-house of his handsome ex-farmhouse in Somerset. I kept by me, as I always do, a book I can dip into if I can't get back to sleep. This time it was ideal, the unexpurgated sixties diaries of Cecil Beaton.

He was a puzzling and interesting man, endearing but irritating, snobbish but denying it, waspish yet unsure of himself, desperate when a lover dumped him to go back to America, a royal fan yet sympathetic towards the young and their work, a friend of Mick Jagger (not for nothing was he satirized as Rip Van Withit); a workaholic (nasty but sometimes accurate word), yet, mysteriously, often broke. But the passage in the diaries which fascinated me most was the revelation that he had at the time suffered from the same diarrhoetic disorder as I did, the trots – the bum-clutching, the explosions, the social embarrassments.

He put it down to overwork and exhaustion, perhaps correctly. Once, the equivalent of my V & A experience, he was forced to evacuate the contents of his bowels on one end of a Parisian seat in a public park At this point I felt total identification with this fastidious dandy. In the end, though, he recovered.

I'm finished now with shitting and pissing, unless either of them have a part to play in the dance of my eventual terminal appointment in Samara.

6. The Fairies and the Goblins

> I told him very loud and clear
> I went and shouted in his ear.
> Lewis Carroll

Now the smelly goblins must give way to the malicious and ever-active fairy-brain surgeons in their war with my mind and vocabulary, with forgetting what I'm looking for and the names of people I've just met or known for ages. Young people will, I guess, groan, if indeed they are reading this at all, and mumbling 'boring old fart' reach for their mobiles, especially if they have a grandfather or ageing relative who bangs on endlessly and repetitively about their experiences during the Blitz. But for those of middle age who can remember the eldritch wail of the sirens night after night, and especially those who still have most of their marbles but are beginning to recognize the slow but steady attentions of the fairies and goblins, and the possibility of being mugged by the demons of the heart attack or the stroke waiting in the wings, I hope it will at least give them the comfort of knowing they are not alone as they enter the shadow of the valley of death. First among my reminders of eventual oblivion is my escalating deafness. Like gout, shingles or piles, but unlike blindness, deafness is considered a more allowable subject for jokes.

Here's an example. Two men were sitting together in a

public house, one deaf, the other not. It was the deaf man's turn to buy a round. On reaching the bar he ordered two pints. After a lot of shouting on the part of the barman, this was established.

'How much?' asked the deaf man.

'Six pounds,' was the eventual demand, grasped by the deaf man only when six fingers were held up to confirm the amount.

'That's a lot for two pints,' said the deaf man as he opened his wallet. The barman acknowledged that it was, but pointed out it was to pay for the entertainment.

'The what?'

'The entertainment.'

After a bit, the barman wrote down a fairly complicated explanation.

'Oh, the entertainment,' said the deaf customer, when he'd finally understood. 'What entertainment?'

'Country and Western,' yelled the barman. The deaf man seemed to hear that.

Returning to his friend, he put down the drinks, complaining that they had cost six pounds. The other man was appalled. 'Six pounds!' he said, in that not especially loud but slow and clear enunciation which, in a man's voice at least, is more effective than escalating shouting. 'Why six pounds?' He only had to repeat it twice.

'To pay for the entertainment,' his friend explained.

'What entertainment?' his mate demanded (three repetitions were needed this time).

'Some cunt from Preston,' was the explanation.

Now, deaf as I am, I find this funny, whereas '"I see," said the blind man, who couldn't see at all', while true enough, is sad. I knew an admirable British jazz pianist who was blind and was led about by a devoted dog called Max. Max led him on to the stage and he sat beneath the piano until he'd finished. Max also looked after him when he was drunk, a fairly frequent occurrence. 'What,' I used to ask myself, 'do blind-from-birth drunks experience?'

Dogs are not only necessary but wonderfully sympathetic companions to their blind owners. I was once asked to present one to its new charge in a distant South London public house. Another blind man there, sitting by his Labrador, told me of an additional advantage. 'People,' he said, 'will come up and pat it and say "What a lovely animal", but they never approach you to compliment you on your white stick!'

I only heard one, for me, acceptable 'blind' joke – hopelessly non-PC but at any rate funny. It was part of the material of the great Morecambe and Wise.

WISE: What would you do if you found a man in bed with your wife?
MORECAMBE: I'd kick his dog and break his white stick!

But deafness? I've been deaf now for many years, although initially only slightly and probably the result of singing in front of quite loud jazz bands. My wife noticed it first as I was increasingly complaining that everybody had taken to mumbling. In the end she insisted I have my ears tested at a surgery famous for its specialization in this area. Emerging from the nearby tube station I discovered on the pavement a series of green-painted footsteps leading to the clinic. This reminded me of the white pebbles dropped by the Babes in the Wood to guide them home if they were lost in the forest. I didn't need them then, nor indeed even now, but I found them both touching and funny.

The doctor tested my hearing, an earplug in alternate ears, a muff in the other, starting with quite loud and deep sounds, but ascending in both tests from a bass note up to a high level, not quite as high as a dog whistle but just as inaudible to me. Afterwards he said, 'Yes. You have what we call ski-slope hearing.' He let me see the chart he'd been marking which showed a fairly steep slope on the graph paper. 'It'll probably get worse,' he said unhelpfully, and indeed it has.

You may wonder, and many have asked, how I can continue to sing. The answer is that most bands these days have monitors, loudspeakers in front of them, so that they can hear what the rest of the band is doing. They are not only adjustable but separate from the house system. However, even without a monitor I can manage. This is because I can hear myself, know my own material, and can take in a considerable part of the musicians' contribution anyway.

A number of other jazzmen have become either somewhat deaf or deafer over the years, but rock-singers, who mostly prefer enormously loud, diaphragm-vibrating amplification, suffer from the effect much earlier. Pete Townshend is a case in point. Jazzbos are lucky in comparison.

So I went a few days later to a private hearing-aid specialist, a very encouraging and jovial man in Harley Street. He too tested me on the 'raise your hand when you can still hear the ascending notes' and then fitted me with a comparatively primitive device with a nozzle which was activated by switching on an adjustable plastic battery on the end of a tube that snaked over the ear.

'Now you'll be able to hear the birds,' he promised and

was proved right, as I walked along Regent's Park looking for a taxi. (Up until then I might have concluded the only birds left were crows and ducks.) On the downside I could also hear traffic but for a bit my wife and friends were equally pleased at the improvement, not only for me but for them too.

That must have been at least fifteen years ago. And indeed it soon got worse. The Harley Street man closed his clinic some time later (a great relief to my budget) and I went 'public'. I saw a doctor at St Mary's Paddington, who sent me down to the technicians' department, 'audiology' it's called, in the basement of another building in that enormous warren I now know so well.

In the interim the devices had improved. They took a cast of both ears and, instead of the teat of yore, produced two snug moulds. Once again the silent hedgerows renewed their song, but finally my hearing began to fade again.

Well, not in all circumstances. In a room with just one or two people, it's not too bad. On the other hand, in a car or taxi in movement, it's pretty hopeless, except at traffic lights (something it often takes some time to convince most cabbies of, who continue to tell, and worse, ask me things while in motion; and despite, usually in the case of older men, being somewhat deaf themselves). But the worst is in situations where there is a loud volume of noise. Pubs, especially with techno and particularly when full of football fans half-pissed because their team has won or lost or, worse still, is winning or losing live on a huge TV, are a disaster. But unless somebody recognizes me and comes up to remind me insistently (and I've usually forgotten) that we met forty years ago, or to ask whether I am still working, or to say they haven't seen me on the box recently (the only *real* proof for many that one exists), I'm in the clear. If not, many refuse to take in that I'm deaf and some take offence, believing I'm faking it (true, I'm afraid, in some cases). Evelyn Waugh, I read somewhere, rejecting hearing aids which, like Picasso and jazz, struck him as 'too modern', relied on an ear-trumpet, but would discard it if bored. Turning off is one of the few bonuses available, but I'd sooner hear properly, of course.

Parties, book launches and gallery openings are imposs-ible, although I still go to some of them for friendly or professional reasons. When approached, my subterfuge is to nod and smile, which usually works, but is a disaster if my interrogator tells me of a crisis in their own lives. Their much-loved mother, they might tell me, has just died, or their husband has an incurable disease. A smile then, still less a remark such as 'You must be pleased', is not what's needed and, if their hurt or angry reaction proves I've put my ear in it, I confess to my deafness, make them repeat what they said until I've understood and apologize profusely. In general, though, I find it better to confess to my disability before they address me, and point at my now two appliances to convince them. Incidentally, few hearing people notice these unless they are whistling, but we, who wear them, take them in instantly.

Another side effect is to mis-hear something and misinter-pret what was said. If I realize that I have misunderstood, I say, 'Surely you didn't tell me' – and then repeat what is clearly absurd. This frequently gets a laugh as I intend. Mostly I get the vowels right, the consonants wrong.

But if what's been said sounds more or less rational, my reaction appears simply dotty. In the early days of John Chilton's Feetwarmers, they kept a small red notebook called

'George's deafies' and when a fair number had accumulated would read them out to me. One example:

THE MANAGER OF THE ADELPHI HOTEL, LIVERPOOL: Mr Melly, is
   your suite comfortable?
ME: What's he want?
MANAGER (*perplexed*): What does who want?
ME: The Chief Constable.

Sometimes these mis-hearings remind me of one of the many games played seriously by the surrealists and guaranteed to produce often apt, yet absurd, results of a certain poetic resonance. An anthology of these seductive distractions is to be found in *Surrealist Games*, a small boxed book published by the invaluable Redstone Press.

Here, with their instructions, are two variants:

One: 'Questions and Answers'. *For two or more players.*

A question is written down, the paper folded to conceal it from the next player, who writes an answer. The paper is unfolded to reveal the result. Remarkable facts result. Here are a couple of startling examples:

Q: What is reason?
A: A cloud eaten by the moon.

Q: Why go on living?
A: Because at prison gates only the keys sing.

The second game, 'The Exquisite Corpse', is, I believe, the progenitor of all the rest. Here are the editor's somewhat longer instructions:

For a minimum of three players.

The players sit around a table and each writes a definite or indefinite article and an adjective, making sure their neighbours can't see them. The sheets are folded so as to conceal the words and passed round to the next player. Each player then writes a noun and conceals it, and the process is repeated with a verb, another definite or indefinite article and adjective, and finally another noun. The paper is unfolded and then read out . . .

It is in effect a variant of the childhood game of consequences. A few examples. The first, by no means the most surprising, but which nevertheless gave the game its name, is

The exquisite corpse shall drink the new wine.

And a sample of others:

The wounded women disturb the guillotine with blond hair.
The avenged topaz shall devour with kisses the paralytic of Rome.

My wife Diana is not only decidedly not a surrealist, but equally is irritated by my 'deafies', although occasionally she is tricked into a frosty smile. I suspect her reason, probably accurate, is that she imagines I exploit them to amuse others, whereas she has been exposed to them for many years. To live with someone deaf is, I realize, a constant strain. We meet largely at suppertime or when we go out together for some joint reason. Insofar as I know, she is never disloyal about me to others except perhaps (pure speculation) her intimate circle of mostly women friends, nor I to her with the same proviso. None the less, my deafness and its concomitant misunderstanding of essential instructions are enough to try her patience. This is how she puts it: 'I have to shout, and it makes me sound bad-tempered and then I *become* bad-tempered!'

This, I can confirm, is true enough.

The malicious fairies of the mind are more insidious than the coarse goblins of the lower intestines and bladder. With great effort they may be kept at bay, but never defeated. Their earliest tactic is the sudden obliteration of names and, less often, of words. There is no time limit here – sometimes I find myself incapable of remembering the name of someone from the distant past, but later, usually in the small hours, it comes to me from the increasingly disorganized filing system of the mind. My favourite comedian of all time, Max Miller – a name, by the way, which has never eluded me – corroborates this. 'Ladies and gentlemen,' he'd confide to the audience, 'I'm going to sing a song I've written. Mind you, it's not finished. I've got the beginning and I've got the end (long pause); it's the middle bit I'm after. It'll come to me in the night (another pause) . . . the middle bit.'

Of course the audience, seduced by the wicked twinkle in his eye and knowing that his meaning was open to sexual interpretation, would begin to laugh. 'No,' he'd repeat, 'in the night, the middle bit . . .'

And then, as was his wont, he'd turn on them for misinterpreting him. 'Go on,' he'd protest in mock indignation. 'Go on, make something of that . . . you filthy lot, you're the sort that get me into trouble . . .'

Oh Maxie! My 'middle bits' are less, far less open to misinterpretation, but none the less irritating.

At parties, however small or large, I often forget the names of two people I know well who are waiting to be introduced to each other. 'You know each other?' I ask them desperately. 'No,' they tell me.

Wally Fawkes, our best classic jazz clarinettist, cartoonist and caricaturist, has a typically throwing solution. He boldly asks them their names, and sometimes, usually with irritation, they tell him. His reaction is extreme congratulatory enthusiasm. 'You're right!' he cries, like a schoolmaster exhilarated by a correct answer from an otherwise dim pupil. 'You're right!' I've tried this gambit but am greeted merely with puzzled irritation. Only Wally can pull it off!

It's not only people who escape through the mesh of my mental net; plays, films, books, much-admired artists, famous jazz musicians may all swim through the wide unravelled holes, even when I knew the exact answer a moment before.

The most worrying manifestation, however, is when the failing mind, like a kind of windscreen-wiper, sweeps across leaving the glass entirely clean to reveal nothing more than a straight road ahead with identical semi-detached houses on either side.

Not long ago I read a newly published novel which, according to Diana, I thoroughly enjoyed. Later, when the *Sunday Telegraph* asked me to name my 'book of the year', I picked it up as though I'd never read it before – I'd seen it all right because my wife had brought it back from the book launch when I was out of London – so I read it, with mounting admiration and enthusiasm, and told Diana it was certainly, despite several other contestants, my choice. Diana said I hadn't reacted quite so positively when I'd first read it. But I had absolutely no recollection of having done so at all – none!

This happens quite often, if not so dramatically. Some of it – 'You never told me that!' 'Yes, I did' – may be due to being increasingly Mutt and Jeff (cockney rhyming slang), but not, as in this case, a whole book!

I used to call it 'the gaslight syndrome'. *Gaslight* was a play, and later on a film, both of which I do remember clearly, about a seemingly lovable but in fact evil husband who wants for his own nefarious reasons to drive his wife mad. One of his means to this end is to turn down the gas pressure in the cellar when she is alone (it's set in late-Victorian times). Happily, insofar as I recall, a friendly detective believes her and unmasks her ingenious tormentor.

In consequence, when confronted by Diana in the past I would suggest that, not only was she lying, but she had adopted the methods of the double-faced spouse.

I no longer doubt Diana. She just rang up from the country to remind me of the time and place of the funeral of a much-loved friend. 'Of course,' she said, 'I told you last week as soon as I'd heard.' I drew a blank but didn't imagine for one moment that she'd crept up from the cellar after interfering with the gas supply.

Names lost. Whole books mentally shredded. And the most irritating aspect is that younger, or at least compara-tively younger people, often assert, mainly I imagine out of kindness, that they share the same handicaps. 'Oh,' they tell me in that special voice they reserve for toddlers and animals, 'I forget *everybody's* name!' It's actually quite annoying. If you are unable to feel tied to age and its tricks, to deafness and its quirks, what's the point of the inconvenience?

My eyesight, on the other hand, while not perfect, is serviceable. The original deficiency was brought about quite a long time ago when the retina in the left eye became detached. The effect of a maverick retina is to make everything waver and sway, producing an effect not unlike the early expressionist German film *The Cabinet of Doctor Caligari*. Everything became wobbly and invisible from certain angles. I consulted a surgeon, a Mr Schonberg, an almost ridiculously handsome and charming man who works part-time at the Western Eye Hospital, attached to St Mary's but facing on to Marylebone Road rather than Praed Street, and just opposite the posh hotel where Miss Day had her farewell party.

Mr Schonberg arranged to sew it back on in the operating theatre but gave me a local anaesthetic, which stung for a few seconds like a bee. It was an odd experience because I could see a bit, but as if through semi-transparent gauze, and could watch his hands in their rubber gloves, holding various, to me, unknown surgical instruments, approaching and receding.

When he'd done, he asked me to stay overnight so he could examine me the next day. In the small hours my sleep was interrupted by a grotesque and comic incident. I was woken by a seemingly indignant Filipino nurse. I couldn't really see her but her rapid Asian voice came from not far above the bed-end and was enough for me to realize that, like many of her compatriots, she was not very tall. What she shouted at me, disgruntled as I was at being woken anyway, was 'How many fingers I got?'

I knew very well what she meant, but felt mischievous. 'Ten, I suppose,' I told her in a measured and reasonable voice.

'I was woken by a seemingly indignant Filipino nurse'

She was gratifyingly irritated. 'No!' she shouted as though to a village idiot. 'How many fingers I got?'

'Oh,' I asked, 'are you one of those people who think their thumbs don't count as fingers? In which case,' I said, 'eight and two thumbs.'

At this answer I feared I might have driven her close to passing out with rage. She tried once more, so loudly I feared she might wake up other patients.

'HOW MANY FINGERS I GOT?' she shrieked.

I decided to relent.

'Oh,' I said. 'Do you mean how many fingers are you holding up?' And I held up several so she knew I was finally on the right track. 'Now, if you'd asked me "How many fingers am I holding up?" I'd have understood at once.'

Finally she relented a little. She felt she'd got through to this dummy. Comparatively calmly she asked me for the final time, 'How many fingers I got?'

I could honestly say I couldn't see any. I told her so and she jotted the answer down on a form and left me in peace.

I'm well aware she was doing her job and I was teasing her. When I saw her in a corridor the next time I apologized for my stupidity, but told her that in the future she could avoid such misunderstandings by saying 'How many fingers am I holding up?' She repeated this several times, but I wasn't convinced that when once again faced by a recumbent patient she would remember. Some time later, asked to speak from a patient's point of view at a gathering of eye doctors and surgeons at the Royal Medical Association building, I told this tale. Their laughter was a sign that they too had encountered misunderstanding resulting from the limited English of nurses from the Philippines, a considerable number, as it happens. Still, without them, without Africans, West Indians and other non-British nursing staff – and doctors, come to that – where would our hospitals be?

The operation was successful, only the two eyes didn't quite work together. Especially when tired, I can see double, not unpleasant in the case of beautiful twins but on balance inconvenient. I therefore tend to sport an eye-patch, especially on stage or TV. This is not entirely necessary but looks, I believe, rather piratical, and as I now sing sitting down, allows me to introduce a joke about a retired pirate king. He had a wooden leg, a hook instead of a hand, and one eye. He spent every night drinking rum at a bar on the Bristol docks. A young seaman approached him one evening and said how much he admired what he had heard of his piratical past, but how, he asked, did he come to lose a hand, a leg and an eye?

'Ar!' said the old salt. 'It were this way, lad. I were boarding a Spanish merchant ship loaded with gold in the Caribbean, when one of they Spaniards brought 'is cutlass down, cuts off my 'and and I falls backwards into the sea.' He took a deep gulp of rum and allowed his young admirer to replenish it. 'Yes, I falls in the sea and a shark 'as me leg.'

'And the eye?' asked his young interrogator.

'Aarr,' said the old man, 'that were different. Some weeks later I were on the poop practising with me wooden leg. I looked up at the sky, a beautiful blue wi'out a cloud in it.' He took another mouthful of rum. 'When a bloody great shite-hawk [naval slang for seagull] did a squit in me eye.' He paused for dramatic effect and then added, 'And I forgets I 'ad a hook!'

Freud thought jokes were to conceal anxieties, and dreams

likewise – he may well have been right. It's odd though that most men like to tell jokes, whereas most women detest them and often don't get them.

Other current failings: going to look for something and forgetting in crossing the room what it was, or, even if I remember it, not seeing it right under my nose. Here, though, there is an odd compensation. Looking for something else I later find, under a chair or on a shelf, glasses, a pen, a book I need that I'd mislaid some time before. I grin with happy relief.

Otherwise I've become clumsy and drop things, breaking them (my mother, who in old age did the same, called it 'the drops'). Like her too, I fart involuntarily. ('Scentless', she'd cry, not always accurately.) Getting out of taxis is especially hazardous. I find it hard, although just possible, to thread a cast or leader through the eye of a fly and to tie the subsequent quite elaborate knot that secures it. And much more.

To return to my eyes, I didn't let drop that my other retina had broken loose some time earlier and been sewn on with immediate success. The second rogue retina came some time later. It was complicated by Mr Schonberg's discovery that I had a 'maculate hole' in the back of the eyeball. Strangely enough my sister Andrée had one of these earlier and came over from France to have it dealt with. I suggested therefore it could be genetic. Impossible, they told me: the chances of developing a maculate hole at all, they said, were very slight. That my sister and I had both contracted them was as likely as winning the lottery. Millions to one!

Mr Schonberg cured mine by replacing the eye's water with oil and draining it off later. It worked but during the treatment the other retina followed the example of its fellow and that needed sewing on again, but why and how had this happened?

I have a possible explanation. Some time earlier I had taken to fainting without warning. I had several things wrong with me; in fact, I was perhaps at my lowest ebb healthwise and had been hospitalized for a chest infection. In falling to the ground, at least twice I had cut my face on sharp corners and on getting up and looking in my shaving mirror, discovered that I had a mask of blood. I stopped bleeding eventually and I cleaned up, but was it possible these knocks and cuts were responsible for the revolt of first one and then the other retina?

Diana keeps her own perfect eyes on me and ensures that I take my pills. Like my hero Luis Buñuel, I have learnt the importance of establishing a strict routine and of not feeling guilty about sleeping, if possible and especially when at Ronnie Scott's, at least twelve hours a day. The medical specialists probe, prod, X-ray and scan me an enormous amount. I walk with great care, especially in stepping over curbs, and if there are no banisters I seek a helping arm. Still, all in all, I think I'm in quite good nick.

7. 'George Melly – God Help Us!'

The world's jazz-crazy, Lord, and so am I –
Old jazz vaudeville song

It was in the sixties, after I'd officially retired from the jazz world, that Wally 'Trog' Fawkes, for whose famous strip cartoon *Flook* I had been contributing the words for almost fifteen years in the *Daily Mail*, let drop that every Sunday morning in a big shabby pub near King's Cross, the mysteriously named Merlin's New Cave, a band made up in the main of retired jazz musicians gathered for a blow.

So, the following week, my TV column safely 'put to bed' in the *Observer*, I cruised down the hill from Camden Town on my moped to suss it out.

They blew in a large room off the bar. You could drink there, but there was no alcohol actually on sale, and this meant you could bring your children with you to tumble about, and the family atmosphere was very sympathetic. The music was not 'trad' but a less rigid form of jazz which, with the recent triumph of rock 'n' roll, I hadn't heard for almost a decade, a music fulfilling the great Jelly-Roll Morton's definition many years before, 'hot, sweet, plenty rhythm'.

The house band, as it were, were called The Chilton-Fawkes Feetwarmers. (The Feetwarmers was the name of a band from the past led by Sydney Bechet, a favourite of both the leaders.) Wally played mostly clarinet. Indeed, Bechet had once declared him the best on that instrument not only in Europe, but in the world, and had asked Wally to join him. Wally, however, weighed things up. He was beginning to establish himself as a cartoonist; he had great talent there and opportunities too. A life on the road with the notoriously moody Bechet, and the conceivably transient popularity of jazz itself, were both factors; he returned to Fleet Street, but has continued to play when and where he chooses to this day.

There was Bruce Turner, a fine saxophonist and famous eccentric, who was still a professional; a non-drinker or smoker, but with a passion for chocolates and cream cakes, a gentle man but a convinced Stalinist, a public-school boy (Dulwich) and yet devoid of snobbery, totally committed to the pursuit of young women or 'mice', the jazz term for them at that time. 'Must have that mouse, Dad!' was one of his many catch-phrases.

He had created a limited yet unique language of his own. When pleased, 'This is the life I tell 'e'; when miserable, 'Wish I was dead, Dad.' While his use of the word 'Dad' was universally applied to men and women, children and dogs, he himself realized this could present difficulties: 'Went to see my father last week, Dad,' he told Wally. 'Didn't know what to call him.'

This performance, while seductive, seemed a little contrived to me, and his extremely fluent playing, as an American muso didn't hesitate to point out, was at times prone to imitation of American masters, often several within the same chorus. 'What's Bruce Turner sound like?' asked his critic. The answer was in fact very good.

Yet despite all this affectation he was extremely lovable, while his 'little boy lost' appeal and wistful good looks were a triumphant success with the 'mice'.

The third member of the more or less permanent front line was John Chilton, not only a fine trumpet player, but a much admired author of jazz biographies, histories and reference books notable for their impeccable research. His own taste was for the small Harlem swing bands, but he had both knowledge and enthusiasm for every style from early New Orleans to late swing, and enjoyed, while he didn't play, bebop and even had some sympathy for 'Free Form' or 'the New Thing' (however it was then categorized), although I don't think he enjoyed it all that much. It was he who was to turn my life around.

He had played in and led many bands, but lacked showbiz charisma, that exhibitionism which is essential (*vide* Armstrong or Max Miller) to 'lay it on the people', as Pops Armstrong put it. John, bald, pale and with glasses, often seemed almost invisible against a white background, and especially in photographs; yet he had (and has) a wonderful sense of humour, is very well read and knows exactly what works on stage. This, I always felt in our years together, led to a certain Svengali-like tendency, a somewhat commanding officer approach to leading a band. 'Move as one,' he would order us if we had to cross a road.

An independent-minded piano-player once gave in his notice. I asked him why. 'Because,' he replied in his sardonic Scottish accent, 'I can no longer abide yon martinet, baby.'

Mostly I loved John, sometimes I actively disliked him, but I never feared him. In his early drinking days he would suddenly snap and shout at me and I would shout right back. During these rows his eyes would become steely, his face purple. Next day we always made it up. We called such a row 'a purple'.

When we first went on the road, a witty woman friend said to me after a concert with the Feetwarmers, 'John watches you like a ballet mother.' Well, I had become his bread and butter and a fair number of musicians can resent that. Ian Christie, for example, for several years the clarinettist in the Mulligan Band, disliked my habit, during a mildly obscene number of Ethel Waters's called 'Organ Grinder Blues', of imitating a flea-ridden ape during the band choruses, scratching myself and jumping up on a piano stool to pretend to groom Mick's head. This pantomime was very popular with the public, but not with Christie.

'I object,' he snapped one day in his slight Northern accent, 'at earning my living as a musician because you can imitate a fucking monkey!'

My almost weekly appearances at Merlin's New Cave led to an increasing number of paid invitations to work elsewhere: universities, private parties, arts centres and jazz clubs. John and the rhythm section were usually there, Wally on whim, Bruce if he could get it together, Dad. The audience reaction was excellent and I was asked also to appear, for somewhat modest amounts of 'bread', in pubs around London with local trad bands.

I hadn't sung much for most of the sixties, but I began at once to sense what I'd missed. My belief is that when jazzmen or -women retire for whatever reason, they are not free but merely the equivalent of 'recovering' alcoholics. Too much sherry in the trifle and not long afterwards a bottle of vodka is hidden in their underwear drawer or golf-bag pocket – and that was happening to me.

One evening during this transitional period we were invited to do a concert at the Institute of Contemporary Arts, in its comparatively new and very grand premises in The Mall. Among those I invited I included a man I'd met on a talking heads programme on TV and the next person to act as a catalyst in my, by this time, unstable life. His name was Derek Taylor and he became one of my best friends until he died, far too young, of cancer.

Derek was slight, good-looking in a somewhat jumpy way, with abrupt bird-like movements of the head, and sported a little moustache. He came, like me, from Merseyside (Hoylake), which always proved an instant bond. After he'd written a golden review of an early Beatles concert in Manchester (despite being sent there by the *Liverpool Echo*, who employed him at the time, to knock them), Brian Epstein got in touch and asked him to become their PR, and so he did. He travelled everywhere with the Fab Four, and his experience as a press-man enabled him to ward off potential scandals, of which there were plenty. Finally he acted as a go-between when John Lennon and Yoko went to bed together 'for peace' – the 'bed-ins'.

After the Beatles broke up (rather acrimoniously), Derek remained very much in touch. George Harrison became his closest friend, with John Lennon not far behind. Derek was married to a warm and wonderful woman called Joan, also from the 'pool'. Although neither of them was Catholic, they had many children and, by the time I met him, they lived in a large house near Ascot.

Derek was by this time an employee of Warner Brothers

Records UK. His position there was that of a licensed loose cannon, with the power to issue LPs. Quite typically, many of these were rather odd choices – a gentle anthology of readings by the actor John Le Mesurier for instance – but the big bosses in New York and California thought that in Britain, Derek must know what the limeys wanted. In fact they didn't want Le Mesurier, popular as he was for his role in that triumphant TV comedy series *Dad's Army*, or at any rate not in impressive numbers, but now and then one of Derek's stranger ideas struck oil. Later on, for example, in the States, he conceived the notion of contracting the rock singer Harry Neilson, who never performed in public, to record a CD of sophisticated and lyrical songs of the thirties. Its title was that of one of the selections (and a great favourite of the liberal-eared Derek), 'As Time Goes By'. In the event it sold like hot hash cookies everywhere in the world. Derek's WB stock gained many points.

Later, after he signed us up with Warner Brothers, I used to drop in to his office in the WB's building with its carpeting, which, unlike Balmoral's tartan, had a pattern of ovals each enclosing an identical Bugs Bunny chewing a carrot. Derek's own large room, like every room he ever had a hand in, contained full-sized furniture but in the idiom of that owned by the seven dwarfs in Disney's *Snow White*; and on the walls a huge number of images which had amused him, especially if they represented Edward VIII before his abdication. Biscuit tins, coronation mugs and other useless souvenirs of the Duke of Windsor were also in evidence.

A good reason for visiting him was that he was equally addicted in those days to drink as to pot and always made sure that you had a glass in one hand and a spliff in the other, the latter no doubt a legacy of his years with the Beatles. We also evolved our own private language.

There was a species of fairly rich stockbrokers, bankers, etc. who spent their weekends in the Home Counties, discarding their city uniforms for cavalry-twill trousers, hairy shooting jackets and polo-necked sweaters and expensive but apparently well-worn cloth caps. They drove Land Rovers and owned rather promiscuously affectionate Labradors. If it were raining, however, they favoured Barbour jackets and green Wellington boots.

We imagined, perhaps it was even true, that every Sunday morning they'd visit the village pub (The Squires Arms) before lunch. This was a strict ritual. The landlord would greet his regular: 'Morning, squire' (preferably we decided he should be ex-RAF and sport a heavy moustache). After a brief exchange of pleasantries, he should turn and unhook a pewter tankard with the squire's Christian name engraved on it, and enquire: 'The usual?'

It was scenarios like this which gave us the word to personify such people. Certain people were 'squires' on sight, certain attitudes 'squire-ish'. The very word became like a spy's password to signal to each other that one of us had spotted a prime suspect. Raising our glasses to each other, we'd cry, 'Cheers, squire.'

The proto-squire was almost certainly Kenneth More, one of the two male leads in the film *Genevieve*. A hearty vintage-car owner on the Brighton run, his laugh, clothes and competitive banter were squire-like before the event.

Another, although more limited, source of mutual delight we discovered in the George Formby film *Turned Out Nice Again*. George played his usual role as a naive Lancashire lad who comes out on top. He finds himself in a smart London nightclub with some crooks who hope to do him down. To help them they have invited two glamorous girls, but he resists their blandishments. Asked who he is, George, who just so happens to have his uke handy, sings an explanatory song called 'I'm the Emperor of Lancashire'. He passes by a table occupied by a group of Mayfair sophisti-cates, including Garry Marsh, a balding, moustached actor often in George's films, usually as a villain. Here, during a gap in the song, Marsh asks his companion, 'Who's that man who's talking loud? Is he one of the usual crowd?' George naturally enlightens him, 'I'm the Emperor of Lancashire'.

It was, however, Marsh's couplets that hooked Derek and me, especially as, while meant to be posh, the final words of each line are distinctively pronounced in what is now known as Estuary English:

> 'Who's that man who's talking LEOWD?'
> 'Is he one of the usual CREOWD?'

From then on, when we met, or rang each other up, we often began our conversation by quoting a line each of this search for enlightenment. Why did it so amuse us? It wasn't overt snobbery, more that this world of nightclubs was in itself generally tacky and who, come to that, could have been 'the usual creowd'?

George Harrison, 'the other George', as Derek called him, was, it seems, a keen Formby fan, a musical taste he shared with the other Beatles. A proof? If you listen to their recording of 'When I'm Sixty-four', you'll hear one of them, probably Paul, interposing a Formby-like 'tee hee' at the end of a chorus.

In fact, one year 'the other George' and Derek attended the annual meeting of the George Formby Appreciation Society in Blackpool. The society was naturally cock-a-hoop to have attracted a Beatle. Among the attractions was a showing of many of Formby's films where the whole audience played their ukuleles along with him, and there was a concert of imitators – the youngest six, the oldest well over sixty-four.

Derek had accepted my invitation and duly showed up at the ICA. It was mostly completely full of 'its usual creowd' – in this case serious young intellectuals on the cutting edge of culture.

The concert itself was a disgrace. We all got very drunk, and John's arrangements were largely forgotten, even by him. Notes were split ad lib, I swore a great deal and forgot the punchlines of jokes. My bladder that night was distinctly unreliable, forcing me often into the wings to relieve myself, audibly, into a fire bucket.

The audience seemed unfazed, even enthusiastic, perhaps finding nothing odd in discovering that middle-aged men could behave as badly as their young rock heroes. Derek himself must have taken in the drink-induced chaos, but equally recognized the favourable effect it had.

In consequence, a few days later John and I signed a contract to record an LP. For us it was a kind of miracle. Subsequently Derek told us he'd booked a Sunday night at Ronnie Scott's and this amazed John and me even more. Ronnie's, after all, was bop's holy shrine.

*

During the early fifties, like most of my contemporaries who
were fans of revivalist jazz, I would never have crossed the
portals of Scott's, either in Gerrard Street, its original and
fairly squalid small headquarters, or indeed after its move in
1967 to its present and much larger home in Frith Street. It
was after all the birthplace of British bebop, the stronghold
of our enemy. Yet, by the beginning of the seventies our
rigid principles had largely dissolved, and hearing on record
the great American originals and some of their British dis-
ciples who were emerging as formidable exponents of 'the
cool', we began to recognize its qualities and would even
visit the club, although admittedly in my case mostly to hear
singers. So John and I and the rest of the Feetwarmers were
not as petrified as we would have been in the days when
Humphrey Lyttelton was our king. In fact, after some years
and to the disappointment of his committed early fans,
Humph himself had swum into the mainstream 'much to
the anxiety of my agent and bank manager', as he put it.

Even so, we never expected to appear at Ronnie's and
wouldn't have done but for the intervention of Derek Taylor.

The club was packed and drink in huge amounts consumed. Behaviour was both wild and appreciative. It was
also uninhibited. Perhaps the most memorable moment was
when a friend of mine, one of a pair of attractive American
twins, stripped to the waist, unheard of since the days of
Storyville, New Orleans, and put into practice the old blues
injunction to 'Shake 'em but don't break 'em'.

All this was watched with some surprise by Ronnie Scott
and his closest friend and the club's manager, Pete King.
Modern jazz was going through a hard time then, as indeed
were most forms of jazz, and they wondered if perhaps it

'The club was packed and drink in huge amounts consumed'

might be a good idea to try us out in a normal interval spot. In the end they decided to risk it.

Derek was delighted by the evening, but a girlfriend of mine at the time (who was to play an important role in the years to come) had watched and listened soberly. Her name was Venetia and she was, to use the then current jazz slang, a 'posh totty'.

'Wasn't that great?' I asked her. She looked at me quite coldly. 'Wait,' she said, 'until you hear it back!'

She was absolutely right. Derek and his two beautiful secretaries, the small shy one whom I'd nicknamed Snowdrop, and her colleague, the more ebullient blonde, Rose, John and I listened to the tape. The first two tracks were just about passable but only just, the remainder escalating chaos. We all agreed we had to record it again in a studio. Then they dubbed in the wild audience reaction and the result was issuable. Nobody who heard it suspected the deception, a successful example of what later on a man called Terry Brown (a sweet man, now alas in the cold ground) who produced many of our later LPs for Pye used to call 'White Man's Magic'.

Derek was delighted with the finished result and designed the cover with typical impish humour. There were, perhaps still are, in Oxford Street a number of photographers, their work displayed in the windows, mostly photos of Nigerian nurses with their bicycles to send back home, and West Indians in gowns and mortar-boards posing with their BA diplomas, to please and impress their relatives in Kingston and elsewhere. It was one of these establishments we entered and booked a session. Derek's only direction was to ask them to mask all lines and blemishes, which I suspect they'd have done anyway. The result was all he'd hoped. I looked like a painted cadaver after the attentions of Mr Lovejoy in Waugh's cynical Californian masterpiece *The Loved One*.

Derek had it framed within a cover of a particularly unpleasant shade of eau de Nil, gave the album the title *Nuts*, and below the image itself he reprinted what they had suggested on the proof, 'Wouldn't this photograph make a fine enlargement?' Typically he sent the cover to the delighted photographer, who displayed it prominently for a time among the nurses and graduates.

In the UK the recording was heavily publicized by Derek on badges and T-shirts in the approved rock fashion. 'Melly-mania' was the typical legend. It did well, if not sensationally, and he decided on a follow-up album, *Son of Nuts*. For this he hired Merlin's New Cave itself. The cover was a blow-up of the front page of the magazine *Exchange and Mart*. He cut out an irregular hole in this and behind it there was another photograph of me, this time emoting and sweating. It was 'warts and all' time.

Meanwhile we made our first paid appearance at Ronnie's, second on the bill to a celebrated US black modern drummer, Elvin Jones. We got on very well with each other and every night, as he came off stage and we went on, he would embrace me, which, as he was sweating profusely, was a flattering but dampening experience. The audience received us with enthusiasm, so much so that we were rebooked for the following Christmas season. This created enormous interest in the press. I was an established TV and film critic and they were intrigued by my resigning from Fleet Street, as it still was, to revert to the road. In a column in the *Spectator*, for example, an eminent journalist, accompanied by an American woman, reported her as saying, 'Who is this guy? He's like Professor Longhair' (a New Orleans pianist much admired by Paul McCartney, who mentioned him in one of his post-Beatles compositions) 'before,' she added, 'he went serious.'

The season went so well they booked us for next year and, in my case, continue to do so up to the present.

The employees at Ronnie's were less adaptable than the punters. They were so cool that one of them at the front desk, when asked who was on, answered rather disparagingly, 'Oh, some little Dixie group.' On another occasion Venetia, who has never missed an appearance of mine there, arrived a little late and, as I'd asked her to, announced her appearance. The same man, unimpressed by her undeniably upper-class diction, replied by asking, 'What am I meant to do? Jump in the fucking air?' At that time John nicknamed the club 'The Frith Street Charm School'.

Since then, familiarity has bred not contempt but friendly acceptance, especially among the bouncers at the door, all of whom embrace me warmly each year on my first appearance in early December. Pete King too has become a true friend, and although during his lifetime Ronnie would always announce our forthcoming appearance with the words 'and then George Melly – God help us', it was humorously intended, not heartfelt.

Forewarned by our own earlier example, we stayed sober enough during our second recording, this time at Merlin's New Cave, not to have to do it all over again.

Derek had ordered Steve the landlord to provide fish and chips for the full house. This he did, charging for each portion as if it were Beluga caviar.

No doubt WB's paid but Derek noted the outrageous amount. He had the huge bill reprinted and inserted a copy in each album when it was issued. Many of those who bought the LP returned it, explaining there must have been a mistake. Steve the landlord didn't make that kind of mistake and was far from pleased. He was, in both character and appearance, not unlike a slightly dodgy character in Dickens anyway. It took, for example, a long time to persuade him to invest in a new piano or at least a passable second-hand one. The instrument in residence was fit only for the pianistic knacker's yard and those eminent American pianists who dropped in were absolutely appalled by it.

The gents, too, would have been condemned by the Bombay health authorities. I was happily never 'taken short' there, but if I had been and it was too late, you'd hardly have noticed. Still the atmosphere every Sunday was magic, and once, leaving to fulfil an evening engagement, Steve gave us a catering tin of crisps. This was kind of him but later, on the way to Maidstone or wherever it was, one of the band gave a cry of horror. He had just popped in his mouth a mouse's head!

Mouse's head apart (Steve the landlord said he couldn't imagine how it found its way into the box of crisps), Warner Brothers UK didn't stop Derek from promoting our LPs. He organized a series of national tours, and came with us. During this honeymoon period the company laid on limos to carry us to the large theatres and halls where we attracted perfectly respectable audiences and put us up in grand hotels. He himself was at his most mischievous and had us constantly in helpless hysterics.

In Edinburgh, at the North British Hotel at one end of Princes Street, he rang up the hall porter and ordered six hookers. The man didn't know what he meant. Derek explained. The response was appalled. 'This is a respectable hotel,' he was told. 'We dinna supply such a sairvice under any circumstances.' He sounded just under control; perhaps he was a member of the ultra-puritanical Wee Free church.

'Oh well,' said Derek completely unfazed. 'Then send up six chicken sandwiches.'

On that visit to Edinburgh, Derek introduced the concert. Obviously extremely drunk, he stumbled and rambled for what seemed for ever, much to the puzzlement and eventually irritation of the largely jazz-loving audience. We more or less pulled it out of the hat.

Next day, at the hookerless hotel, he sprinkled 'grass' in our Scotch broth. At that time, in the early seventies and beyond, John had a bookshop in Great Ormond Street, run then by Teresa, his short, bright and formidable wife, who had previously retired to give birth to and rear their three children. While jazz books were the staple fare, many of them ordered from the States, there were other general books, some rare first editions, while the regular browsers included many distinguished writers and bibliophiles. In any town we visited John sought out the booksellers (largely an unpleasant race, in his view) to find useful books not only for Teresa's shelves, but also for his own considerable library, often uniform editions of Hardy, Evelyn Waugh and several others to his liking.

On this occasion, unaware of the cause but high as a space probe, he set off and bought, at the full asking price, loads of rubbish; fourth editions of Warwick Deeping, nineteenth-century sermons in Welsh, anything! Later, when the effect of the grass wore off, he wondered if the first shop he entered hadn't alerted the others that there was a free-spending madman on the loose.

And so we hunted the drunken snark, spooning down haggis and neaps and downing rare malts.

It was in Glasgow that Derek's last memorable prank of the tour took place.

He and I entered a pretty tough pub with a crowd of middle-aged drinkers, heavily tattooed, and in some cases bearing facial scars, who looked at Derek with suspicious amazement.

Finally one of them lit his Sweet Afton with a standard lighter. Derek asked to see it. The man reluctantly passed it over. Derek offered him five pounds. 'It's no' worth that,' said its owner.

'Ten then,' said Derek.

While perhaps tempted, the man still resisted. 'It's only an ordinary wee lighter,' he told him.

'Oh all right, thirty, then,' said Derek counting out the notes with a picture of Sir Walter Scott on one side.

This was too much for the owner of the lighter to turn down. Holding the money up to the dim light bulb, he pocketed it and rather aggressively handed over the 'wee lighter'.

After we left we wondered what line their subsequent analysis of this very un-Caledonian demonstration of topsy-turvy anti-business practice might have taken. The landlord, opening many bottles of Wee Heavy, must have been delighted.

*

And so we returned eventually to London. Derek was still convinced he could sell me to Warner Brothers US and later he and I flew over to try to bring this off. He failed dramatically. Meanwhile, despite going professional, work in Britain, Warner Brothers promotions and Ronnie Scott's apart, seemed to dry up. There was less about somehow than even in our semi-pro days.

Ronnie Scott's was not only a club but also ran an agency, upstairs. Although Derek still advised us, it was the Scott Agency who booked or, in this case, didn't book us. We had, as our own agent within the organization, a sweet young man with very long eyelashes called Chips. We liked him very much personally, but began to suspect that, as an addict of both vodka and sleep, he wasn't up to the job. I doubt he lifted the phone very often.

John and I went into Pete King's office to complain about this state of affairs and Pete told us that it was all going to change. 'You'll be working so hard,' he told us in his seductively laid-back East London voice, 'that you won't 'ave time to wipe your arses.'

This just didn't happen. Then, as later, our arses remained as clean as whistles.

Finally John and I decided to resign. We made an appointment and walked into the office at the agreed hour. Pete was there. Chips was there (Ronnie didn't interfere much with business) and another man was there, in his middle fifties so far as I could judge. John and I recognized him at once. His name is Jack Higgins.

Now in his eighties, Jack has had a full and action-packed life. He has a healthy, rubicund complexion and has always dressed smartly, if slightly squirishly. His only physical handicap is his teeth, of which there are remarkably few, clearly by design, for if he wanted he could have easily been fitted with the best on the market, literally 'the cutting edge'. He is a gourmet and wine specialist, an excellent cook even when it is only for his own benefit. He now grows his own vegetables and keeps ducks, named after famous jazz musicians, like Buck (or Duck) Clayton. His voice is classless, his laugh, when he is crossed professionally, is humourless but formidable and has earned him, among those who have opposed his professional propositions or attempted to beat him down financially, the decidedly unflattering nickname 'The Braying Mantis'. While I have occasionally lost a limb in his chomping jaws I remain very fond of Jack 90 per cent of the time. We've never needed a contract.

For most of his adult life Jack has been in the agency business. For many years after the war he was second-in-command to the formidable Harold Davidson, whose agency handled the importation of and the arrangements for American stars from a wide musical spectrum, including jazz and blues. With most of these, he became a friend – but not inevitably. He much disliked Roy Eldrich, for instance, a great if slightly underrated trumpet player, and the bridge between Louis and Dizzy. This, I'd speculate, had nothing to do with Roy's musical prowess, but probably arose from his touchiness and easily triggered temper.

Jack had told me of this antipathy, and as his tales of his early years are completely fascinating, I asked him how he'd got on with the white cornet player Ruby Braff, a notoriously irascible person. Jack often surprises me. 'Perfectly well,' he told me, in a tone of voice indicating that he in turn was surprised at my question. 'He was always completely reliable as to business arrangements.' In fact Jack's measure of a client is neither talent nor genius, although most often this is their selling point, but their professional approach to jobs and money.

Of course, dealing with American stars he has inevitably come into contact with their very tough managements, sometimes, as is widely known and right through from the twenties, connected to the mobs. No bother there of course, but then Jack is physically fearless. Someone told me, it may have been John, that he was in a Soho pub much frequented by villains when a gang fight broke out. No guns in evidence, but knives flashed, and chairs, glasses and bottles flew through the air. John, if it were he, left at once, but glancing back, took in that Cool-hand Higgins, who was sitting at the bar sipping a half pint, didn't move a muscle but observed the whole fracas like an entomologist might a war between red and black ants.

So what was Jack L. Higgins doing in Ronnie Scott's office? He had for some years prior to this unexpected appearance managed a marina, but now, snorting like the war-horse in the Old Testament 'Ha! Ha! Amongst the trumpets', felt a need to return to the music business. Pete King, perhaps not unaware that that branch of the business was not the jewel in the Scott crown, had, when Jack applied, taken him on.

Pete had told Jack that we were coming in to see him about something and Jack, having looked at the snow-blinding almost empty date-sheet, predicted we were going to resign. Pete said he couldn't believe *that*, but Jack said he was sure.

He had then taken the no-doubt-reluctant Chips into another office with a telephone and, although, as a recent member of staff, he was the more junior employee, made him ring up jazz clubs and other modest venues all over the country.

When John and I came in, our determination reinforced by a couple of drinks in the Intrepid Fox on the corner, we began to say something like, 'No offence, Pete, but . . .' when Jack strolled forward and handed us both sheets of paper. 'Your date-sheets for the next month,' he told us in a throw-away voice. While admittedly in most cases modestly rewarded, almost every night was booked!

From then on Jack raised our fees where possible, but his personal intentions were less in evidence. He learned all he could about the current jazz world; he had a fast memory; and he was prepared to stay in the office until long after Chips had left to relax even further, or perhaps kip.

Then, when he was good and ready, the long green legs rubbed together and the harsh laugh of the Braying Mantis was heard in the land. Jack Higgins resigned; and shortly afterwards he asked us to join him.

Pete was furious. The scales fell from his eyes once he had understood Jack's strategy. He refused to speak to him for many years and the negotiations for our Christmas appearances at the club had to be conducted through a third party in Frith Street. (Chips had left shortly after Jack's defection.) Jack was refused entry to the club on Pete's instructions, even in the company of friends, for many a season. Recently, however, they communicated again – another great, if on this occasion pleasant, surprise for me.

Pete, however, in no way tried to dissuade John and me

from joining Jack's new agency, with its smart office in Charing Cross Road.

And so we continued to play at Ronnie's, when the stupid lights come on each year in Oxford Street, and Soho is suddenly one-way and almost impenetrable. For John most likely, for me certainly, our first appearance had been something of a miracle. Since I'd been a jazz-hooked adolescent I had dreamed of singing into the small hours in a famous appreciative jazz nightclub and being driven home in a taxi through the almost empty streets. Now, with what the surrealists called 'the certainty of hazard', it was happening – and still is!

8. Up at Ronnie's

I have appeared for over thirty years at Ronnie Scott's, that is to say over a third of my life, covering my involuntary arrival in the suburbs of old age and fairly soon, I fear, the city centre itself.

For those who have never visited the club (those who have may skip this passage, as no description can cap the reality), you enter under a neon sign through two big glass doors. You arrive in the comparatively large expanse of the lobby. It holds on the right a desk where you can buy or book your tickets and order a taxi (not always instant). Then, a low table with an unexpected vase of beautiful flowers, and a leather sofa and armchair. On the other side of the foyer, round the corner, is a cloakroom, and then a doorway and staircase down to the loos and the downstairs bar.

This area is policed by a number of minders. 'Policed' is too stern a word – they are in general welcoming and of considerable charm. After so long they have become my friends, especially their 'captain', a big, handsome bearded man with a deep and beautiful voice, and we embrace every night.

My only occasional difference of opinion has been with the doorman. If the club is full and the street holds many people who hope for returns or the chance to stand at the bar once those who have booked are seated, he lets them dribble in, cold and, if it's raining, damp too. I am allowed a certain number of guests and invariably leave their names both at the desk and with the competent and beautiful young woman who holds an identical list and shows guests to their tables. *But* the doorman has no such list and quite often during our last gig my guests, despite protesting, were stuck out there for ages too. The doorman complains they don't let him have a list. They say they do. Well, next Christmas I'll get it sorted.

There were many quite comical clashes between staff and punters in those early days, perhaps understandably in that most of the former were convinced bop-lovers, the apotheosis of 'cool'. (Not a new word at all, kids. It was coined to establish the difference between what the boppers were playing and the 'hot' jazz which preceded them.) Well, today the bitter war has ended in a sort of truce: all schools, or most of them, admire the masters of mainstream.

Up a few steps and you come into the main body of the club itself, a fair-sized room with pink shades low over the tables – indeed the general effect is of the colour rose. There are tables of different sizes covered in dark red cloths, some suitable for a couple, others which can accommodate six or more. It's quite dark and the serving staff use torches to illuminate the usually reasonable bills. The artists are picked out by spotlights.

In front of the stage is a no-smoking well. Behind it, raised behind a brass rail, is the main seating area, leading right back almost to the entrance wall. To the right and left are two smaller seating areas, the one on the left backed by the long bar individually lit, and on the right an area known rather unfairly perhaps as 'the graveyard', although if seated there you can see the musicians in profile.

Behind the stage is the artistes' rather cramped dressing-room with a chaise longue and several chairs. There is a sink and, up a few stairs, a loo. For a long time this housed only an Elsan. Then it was locked (health inspectors?) and most of us, if not fanatically fastidious, in an emergency used the basin, with the exception perhaps of the great and alas late Ella Fitzgerald. Finally, along a short corridor, is the rather cluttered office with a big desk behind which sits Pete King, looking magisterial but usually friendly like a good guy in Dickens. There are TV sets in both dressing-room and office.

There is, of course, a sound and lighting cubicle, and on stage stands a very grand and frequently tuned piano. The walls throughout are a collage of framed photographs. I can't think of anything I've left out except that, after the club shuts at three, they turn on the full bare-bulbed lighting system to drive out the few punters reluctant to leave. It's so depressing it usually works. I think all clubs are like old tarts, sad under full lighting. John Betjeman wrote a poem about one. It began

> I walked into the night-club in the morning;
> There was kummel on the handle of the door.

I've encountered no kummel, except behind the two bars in a bottle, but he's caught the rather depressing, brightly lit ambience perfectly.

To pin down the audience at Ronnie's is impossible, in that it depends on who is appearing. If the music is avant garde it draws serious musicians and some rather sparse fans who listen intently so as to grasp and understand what they are hearing. A mainstream attraction fills the club with those who, as adolescents, wound up their gramophones to listen with admiring attention to the innovative masters of their youth. As for classic bop, its public are those who were originally drawn to Charlie Parker and his ilk in the early forties.

And us? Well, we are the only representatives of what the bald midget at the desk called 'some little Dixie group', not that either John Chilton or Digby Fairweather would thank you for that. 'Dixie' John's quartet was indeed small, but for Digby, with seven musicians including himself, that 'little' is surely an understatement.

The Christmas season fills Soho with ravers of both sexes and quite a number stagger into Ronnie's, which is open late. There are office parties too, youngsters whose parents or even grandparents talk warmly of me, and above all, contemporaries or near-contemporaries who often open a conversation with the dread phrase, 'I haven't seen you since . . .' As 'since' tends to be far away and long ago, I use John's mild put-down (although with a friendly smile), 'You didn't like it much, then?'

This audience can be volatile and thoughtless and in the past those who want to hear have frequently complained about the steady volume of conversation (being deaf I was less aware of it), but I must say now that I sit in a chair to sing at them, they have become in the main much quieter.

There are exceptions, of course. The night the din drove the already depressed Ronnie from the stage at the beginning of his jokes was one such, but it can be handled. John Chilton gave a devastating riposte to a single lout shouting the odds: 'Don't pay any attention. It's his first visit to London and he is over-excited by the big red buses.'

These days I have evolved my own formula for vocal mayhem. I start off by saying, 'This is not a church. There is no reason why you shouldn't talk, but I would like to remind you that most of the audience have paid to listen to the music, so I would ask you to do it quietly. There is also a downstairs bar opposite the ladies, where you can talk as loudly as you like. Now I have no power or right to enforce my request, but if you choose to ignore it, well FUCK YOU!'

I only had to resort to this once in 2003, but what was very encouraging was that the majority of the audience burst into prolonged applause and it did the trick. It may have had something to do with me being old and wearing an eye-patch, or having been described by the *Daily Express* as 'a national treasure' and elsewhere as 'a legend' (I thought legends had to be dead, but no matter), or the fact that someone so old and crumbly could shout a four-letter word at them, or perhaps my singing had improved. Certainly another factor is that Digby and his Hot Six are all fine musicians playing their leader's arrangements with complete conviction and swinging like the clappers. At all events, for the rest of both sets you could hear a pin drop. (Where did that cliché come from?)

Ronnie himself was not above a critical reaction but it was usually directed at the artistes he'd booked rather than at the noisy audience. One such was an excellent jazz cabaret singer and pianist called Blossom Dearie. Ms Dearie is a diminutive blonde of a certain age with a quiet, high-pitched voice and great determination in getting her own way. Her material is both literate and sophisticated – my favourite is a song called 'Bernie My Attorney' about her gay lawyer –

'The audience burst into prolonged applause . . . It may have had
something to do with me being old and wearing an eye-patch'

but she insists on certain rigid conditions. One is no smoking during her act – not unreasonable for a singer. Ella Fitzgerald also insisted on it. Two is total silence all the time she is on stage. This, at Ronnie's, is more difficult to fulfil, and one night she blew her top. Stopping in mid-number, she squeaked indignantly at the audience, 'If you go on talking I'm heading straight back to New York!'

Ronnie happened to be leaning on a brass rail at the back of the club in the dark. In the silence that followed this rather child-like tantrum he said in a matter-of-fact voice, 'There's a plane from Heathrow, Blossom, very early in the morning.' She carried on playing and singing.

The only other time he intervened was when Pete rang him up in Australia where Ronnie was on tour, to complain about the behaviour of the current attraction, Nina Simone. She was in my view a great artiste, a fine composer, vocalist and pianist. She had a lot of the power of Bessie Smith, my passion; and indeed used to sing one of that diva's most yearning numbers, 'I Need a Little Sugar in My Bowl'.

The night I went, she sang two full sets, and I was much moved. It was, as is always the case, a full house, many of the audience tough little dykes in jeans and bovver-boots. She had become, it seems, a lesbian icon.

Other evenings were apparently less satisfactory. Sometimes she didn't show up at all. Sometimes she walked on stage in her street coat carrying large shopping bags and sang very few numbers. Once she didn't perform but instead harangued the audience for being white.

So Pete rang Ronnie and asked him what to do. 'Sack her!' said Ronnie from Sydney. I didn't envy Pete this task.

He was, after all, white and Ms Simone when roused had the temper of an angry rhino. But it had to be done.

In our early days at the club both John Chilton and I drank at times heavily, and although John kept it under control on stage, I less so. Indeed, one night I passed out half-way through the first set and finished up under the piano. John addressed the audience: 'The Captain,' he told them, 'is no longer in charge of the ship.'

A season later, during our break the door to the dressing-room opened precipitately and a young, slightly pissed, natural blonde with long hair staggered down the few stairs. She had big shoulders, the result, perhaps, of driving a van for a South London building firm and later for the council, a minute waist and long legs. She was in every respect a tired businessman's dream au pair girl. She made it quite explicit that she wanted fucking. The band tactfully withdrew, probably to the downstairs bar, and – hardly believing my luck – we set about it.

Later, though, Pete pulled me up. 'Look, George,' he said mildly, 'don't shag birds in the dressing-room.' How did he know? I don't think there was a hole in the wall or a two-way mirror. I'm sure there wasn't a camcorder and I don't in any way suspect any of the band of sneaking. However, I never did it again – not in the dressing-room, that is.

At the end of the evening Heather was waiting. She had her little van and we drove into a dark cul-de-sac off Tottenham Court Road, far enough from Pete's X-ray eyes. We'd just got going when a torch came on. 'It's the fucking law,' she whispered. The copper wasn't too officious. 'Not in my manor,' was his only request, so we drove towards

Camden Town where I then lived and climaxed triumphantly behind the Black Cat factory.

The following day, Sunday, I had the day off and Heather turned up mid-morning to check I was OK. Much to my delighted surprise she pulled off her jeans and got into bed in her socks (one of my fetishes). From then on we had a long affair until she fell in love with a big bearded man for whom I guaranteed a motor bike. Of course he didn't keep up the payments and I got a threatening letter about it, but Heather stepped in and made him pay up. As a socialist she had a persuasive moral streak in this direction.

After they'd gone off together – Vroom! Vroom! – she still came to visit me for a bit, but then backed out. I asked her why. 'I guess I love the guy,' she told me à la Billie Holiday.

Before this doleful event we had a sexual and personal ball. She was full of fantasies, for example that I was a rapist. She would pretend to be praying. I would burst in, throw her on the bed and 'have my way with her'. She once asked me to do this on Hampstead Heath, but here I refused on the grounds that she might be unable to resist shouting successfully for help. Might she be unable or unwilling to explain it away? Would I be branded a real rapist, even if she refused to charge me, as I'm sure she would have? I am not a rapist, although on a few occasions, usually frustrated by brewer's droop, I have got a bit violent.

We did it everywhere. In the loo of a train going to Nottingham for example. When we came out there was a rather seedy middle-aged man waiting. He said he was a BR detective and was going to report us. 'Bollocks!' said Heather. ''E's a wanker!' and so it turned out. A ticket inspector told us he was constantly trying this on, but it was difficult to charge him as most couples would be too embarrassed to press charges. We did see that and, while not embarrassed, felt it would waste a great deal of time.

It was in fact in a rather grand hotel in Nottingham that Heather and I experienced our most prolonged and ecstatic night of love/lust. She had brought some powdered speed and we didn't stop until dawn. In the bed, on the carpet, in the shower – it was amazing.

She could behave badly. Once in a North London pub when John introduced me as 'the wisest of all the entertainers – the most entertaining of all the wise men', she, quite drunk, shouted out very loudly, 'No 'e fuckin' isn't.'

She took a certain pleasure when builders on scaffolding wolf-whistled at her and sometimes asked what she was doing with an old cunt like me. 'Is 'e very rich?' they'd shout, or 'Is 'e fuckin' famous?' Actually, for I had become much better known again since going back on the road, she said she had preferred it when she'd first seen me at the Osterley Rugger Club jazz nights and I was more obscure. She was not alone in this preference. All my partners tended to share this view. After first enjoying being in the company of a minor celeb (how I hate that silly word!), they got to dislike being ignored and pushed aside by fans or anyone else who recognized me or even *thought* they recognized me.

Heather was not a gold-digger. Her strong anti-bourgeois principles were set against chic restaurants which I rather enjoy. She'd go to the pictures but refused the theatre as 'a bourgeois spectacle', a view also held by André Breton, the Pope (or Saint) of surrealism. I did, however, persuade her to go to see Alan Bennett's *Habeas Corpus*. She sat there stony-faced until Alan, as a charlady, rushed about the set with a phantom vacuum in his hands shouting 'Hoover! Hoover! Hoover!' Suddenly she couldn't stop laughing. But it didn't mean conversion.

She was quite promiscuous, a vice I've always found provocative, and now and then would bring a boy or girl-friend to share our bed, although usually, I have to say, to their indifference or embarrassment.

She wasn't greedy. In the several years we were together she allowed me to buy her a fun-fur, and a small second-hand van. She could be, and was, jealous of another girlfriend of mine who was equally jealous of her. As for me, I have never felt even a twinge of jealousy except for a compara-tively short time when dumped.

A final possibly unexpected fact about Heather. She had been for a time at art school and drew and painted small watercolours that, while not outstanding, showed some talent. Her calligraphic handwriting was immaculate.

It may seem to some readers that the last episode is simply pornographic. I have no regrets about writing it, but equally I had, before I wrote it, no intention of, literally, 'banging on'. It just took over, due, I suspect, to my now total physical impotence, but still actively erotic imagination.

I had a dear friend, a painter called John Banting. He was both a surrealist and, for a long time, a communist, a combination that Breton refused to accept after the Soviet show trials during the thirties, let alone the murder of Trot-sky, but perhaps John had resigned or no one told 'the Pope'. He also despised high society and caricatured it brilliantly in his *Blue Book of Conversation*, yet he was, during the thirties at any rate, welcome in *haute bohème*. As a young man, broken nose and all (perhaps especially on that account), he was madly fond of fucking, largely, but not exclusively, men. He was a great favourite among gay aristocrats, and indeed one of them left him an annual allowance on which he lived in his old age, as by that time whiskey had destroyed his ability to offer anything beyond scribbles. Earlier he had real talent, especially as a decorator, and he also painted stylized but effective portraits.

One of John's great virtues was his faithful friendship with those once glittering figures who, in their senility, through drink and possibly drugs had become non-sortable. Bryan Howard himself was one such and so was Nancy Cunard, a hopeless wreck living in a squalid cottage in the West Country, and who I believe died in his arms.

John himself, a man without sentimentality, had moved from London in the fifties to a dusty flat in Hastings high above the sea. It was in a terrace called White Rock Gardens, but he called it Rock and Roll Gardens. It was full of tryfid-like plants which had almost taken over. Here and in the nearby local he drank an enormous quantity of whiskey, keeping pace with his final partner (as they call lovers these days), an elderly piss-artist called Jim whom I always thought was a Scot but who turned out to be an ex-Devon fisherman. He was usually remarkably silent, hence perhaps my geographical error.

John remained a surrealist in spirit. He wore at all times a pair of dark blue gymshoes with toes painted at the front end in imitation of *The Red Model*, a picture on this theme by René Magritte. I visited Rock and Roll Gardens quite often because I appeared nearby in the early seventies with a band called Brian White, at the Caravan Club at the end of the front. John and sometimes the silent ex-fisherman usually came with me together with that great and still vastly underrated artist the late Edward Burra, who lived not far along the coast at Rye. Dusty-looking and crippled from childhood with arthritis (how did he paint those large, immaculate watercolour washes, those hallucinatory details?), he was a witty and malicious companion speaking exclusively, for he was of respectable upper-middle-class origin, in what was known in his youth in the twenties as 'Mayfair cockney', and made him and his friends whom I later met sound like old Edwardian tarts. He had the ability to transform anywhere he entered – a gay pub full of trans-vestites or, in this case, the Caravan Club – into one of his satirical paintings.

The boss of the club wore one of those evening-dress shirts with ruffles down the front edged with purple. His wife was a wonder. She complained that Biba's, at that time a big department store in Kensington High Street, made wonderful clothes but only for the skinny young, none for what she called 'the fuller figure'. The shoes, though, were another matter. She'd buy a dozen pairs at a time.

Burra, a keen aficionado of footwear, said to me, 'She wants you to look at her feet, dearie – they are very small!'

Ed Burra and John used to roam Hastings Old Town together and Ed had developed an almost teenage liking for pot. Ed's life, his foreign travel, the excessive drinking and taste for very strong spicy food were unwise, given his physical frailty, and he was sometimes quite ill, but he always seemed to recover. He and Banting used to 'raid' London from time to time, and once came to see me in Camden Town. On the wall of the living-room hung a large and beautiful post-war painting of Ed's. It was a red, erect and phallic railway cutting plunging into a tunnel in a gentle feminine Kent landscape. He never mentioned it or seemed to notice it. He hated to discuss 'Fart' as he called it. Yet I was very impressed when he told me that during his stay in Harlem in the twenties he had heard the great Bessie Smith – not that he expressed any great enthusiasm. He compared her to a London hostess of the time, 'poured into a maroon dress'. He loved jazz, however, and black people too – many of them appeared in his paintings throughout his long career.

I don't think he had any sex life, due to his physical disability and especially an enormous and rather appropriate spleen, and this helped him work and produce a formidable body of paintings and drawings. He never judged except in the case of pomposity and dictatorial behaviour. He gave me a 78 rpm vaudeville blues record which perfectly summed up his sophisticated enthusiasm for 'doing your own thing'. It was called 'A Green Gal Can't Catch On'. To hear him pronounce it in his usual Mayfair cockney was a hoot.

John, on the other hand, kept his sex life going as long as he could, but when I asked him in his comparatively old age if he was still active, he sadly admitted he could no longer do it. As he put it when we passed some very beautiful hippies in the Old Town, 'I can only fuck them with my eyes!'

Today, over twenty years later, I am forced to give the same dispiriting response.

Although he'd written to tell me he was in hospital, John hadn't even hinted it was terminal and that he would never go back to Rock and Roll Gardens, so I didn't go down to Hastings to see him before he died. His remarkable lesbian lawyer, a very twenties figure, wrote to tell me he'd left everything, except for a picture to each of his executors, to the almost silent Jim. John's executors turned out to be Roland Penrose and myself. We had long been non-speakers, but I'd always secretly liked him and we were delighted, without reproach on either side, to make it up.

Jim sat, even more silent than usual, in his chair, a half bottle of whisky (Haig) to hand, while Roland and I tore up a great many drunken scribbles which would have done John's reputation, such as it had become, no favours, and kept everything else. Jim said nothing, but when we uncovered a rather good portrait John had painted of him as a handsome, butch young seaman (do I imagine a tattoo?) we asked him if he would like to keep it.

'Sell everything,' he mumbled.

In effect there was not that much to sell except, among the books, an enormous volume of black prose and poetry edited by the negrophile Nancy Cunard during the Harlem renaissance. It was not only a beautifully edited and printed book but, being rare and in this case warmly dedicated to John, extremely valuable. I was tempted but couldn't. Even if a built-in bourgeois inhibition against stealing hadn't prevented me, the sad stocky figure of Jim slumped in his chair, whom we had to move about like a piece of furniture, would have stopped me.

I chose two small, same-sized, rather good coloured drawings of the *Blue Book of Conversation* period, but, possibly as a symbol of our renewed friendliness, or perhaps because both his farm at Muddle's Green and his flat in Kensington were crammed with cubist and surrealist masterpieces, Roland gave me his too. It was, as Bogart says to the

French police chief (or was it vice versa?) at the very end of *Casablanca*, 'the start of a beautiful friendship'.

There was quite a lot of money in John's bank account and Jim kept it there, like a squirrel, and lived off the state in an old people's home. When he died some years later, I got a letter from Dyke and Co. telling me that Jim had left everything to my children. This surprised me and delighted them, because Jim, just before he went into the home, had played me a mean trick. A girlfriend of mine, a Courtauld graduate, had proposed we write a book on John together and she'd gone down to Hastings to do some research and, in the pub round the corner from Rock and Roll Gardens, the regulars had told her that, Roland being dead, I had personally robbed Jim of every penny John had left him. I now suppose this was because he felt nervous that the money in the bank, which he never touched, might come to the attention of the tax authorities, who'd take most of it and deprive him of his place in the old people's home.

My girlfriend, however, was furious in my defence and, being a formidable no-holds-barred advocate, convinced them that Jim had done me an injustice.

When he died and I found out about his act of perplexing generosity (he'd never even met my children), I felt in fairness I should go down to Hastings to attend his funeral. The congregation consisted only of some staff from the hospice and myself. As is often the case, the vicar asked me, for I was early, if I could give him any personal details because he hadn't known the deceased, the lover of Banting and Haig whisky, the hider of the nest-egg. I wasn't much help to the vicar on this occasion.

After the bleak ceremony, the representatives of the home

asked me back for biscuits and sherry. They were a jolly lot and the place seemed to be run on admirably liberal lines. There was, for example, a smoking room and, if physically capable, the inmates could walk down the hill to a nearby pub. Of course all this permissiveness was years before Nanny Blair began to treat us as if we were all in old people's homes ourselves – but of the old-fashioned, rule-bound, 'matron-knows-best' variety.

I asked about Jim. 'No trouble at all,' they told me. 'But he kept himself to himself, no friends or confidants among the other old people; a loner.' That was about what I'd have expected. I left in good spirits. This lively place seemed a great improvement on the grim names of its equivalent in pre-war Liverpool. 'The Home for Incurables' (Protestants), 'The Hospice for the Dying' (Roman Catholics).

With Heather now living in Teddington and John, Jim and Ed Burra dead, I almost decided to cut the former back down to our reproached coupling on the floor of the band's dressing-room at Ronnie's, and to leave out the latter trio altogether. But then I thought, this last section does at least demonstrate how us oldies bang on, leaving the main road and finding ourselves totally perplexed as to where we were originally aiming. For instance, I have several contemporaries whom I visit fairly often for a few days, like those Edwardian maiden aunts who filled their declining years with a fixed round of country-house visits. And what do we talk about?

We have two main topics: an almost competitive analysis of our individual health and its treatment (I take more pills than you do) and our erotic memories of long ago ('Down

Mammory Lane', as one of my old mates once described it).

I believe that the latter is not so much to try to stimulate our fading libido but to reassure us on a 'but Jenny kissed me' level that we were not always just 'dirty old men' but dirty young ones too, and to remind ourselves that some of the nice old ladies who come up to me after concerts knew us when we were young and raunchy. If we retain any sense we will avoid flirting, remembering that the very idea of randy old tortoises is repulsive to anyone we might fancy, and besides I'm completely impotent and, even if I weren't, am sexually indifferent to those of my age group, although a few of them very occasionally indicate they might be persuaded to take up where we left off.

The poet and critic Al Alvarez once wrote that one summer's day he and a contemporary were chatting amicably on Hampstead Heath when two ravishing girls in their late teens walked by. He and his chum automatically chirped up, adjusted their body language and, while appearing not to notice the girls, presented themselves as possible prospects. No way! The nubile pair didn't so much look through them as make them feel totally invisible.

When I hobble on stage these days and sit down to sing, I open my set, not with John Chilton's 'Good Time George', which he wrote for me about thirty years ago, but Hoagy Carmichael's 'Old Rockin' Chair'. Far more appropriate now. After that I gaze into the auditorium or club. 'I can remember a time,' I tell the audience, 'when I used to look at you and wonder not just whether, but which – No more!'

But now, after this fairly convincing demonstration of my inability not to indulge in involuntary repetitive anecdotes as the shadows grow longer, back to Ronnie's and last year's season.

It was much as usual. There were no disasters, although once, fuelled by Jameson and Digby by vodka, I became pompous in bringing up things I felt might be mutually improved and he reacted by pointing out that after all it was *his* band. Next day, though, we rang each other up, eager to apologize first.

This was Digby's second year (2004) at Ronnie's and he is still amazed at being there and to such a warm reaction. It was my thirty-first year at the club but I'm just as thrilled as he is. For me it's the sense of sharing the 'green' (green-gage = stage) with an impressive number of past jazzmen and -women. As a small sample (a full listing would cover about six pages): Count Basie, Ben Webster, Don Rendell, Coleman Hawkins, Ella Fitzgerald, Max Roach, Milt Jackson, Eddie 'Lockjaw' Davis – and of course Ronnie himself.

My long years there with John Chilton's Feetwarmers, including our last season together, were equally exciting for me, but not for him. Tired and nervous, he was longing to retire and about to do so. For him Ronnie's was already in the past, but not for me.

In our break Digby and I go down to the bottom bar, quite often accompanied by his friend Lisa, who is a wonderful businesswoman and a brilliant grafter at selling CDs and books, which we sign. I have a blank piece of paper for people to write their names down so I can spell them correctly as otherwise, being so deaf, I would quite often get them wrong. In John's day, although he sometimes did it himself, usually a member of the band was paid to take Digby or Lisa's place.

Of course, this Kasbah-like activity leaves us exposed not only to nice people, many of them younger than you'd expect at Ronnie's, who simply want to say how much they enjoyed it, and others whose parents or even grandparents were or had been fans of mine, but also to bores, and drunken bores at that.

Last year, for instance, as you've read, I went to see Conroy, who had just become physically and mentally ill, in an annex of the Hampstead Royal Free Hospital. Emerging, rather depressed, I was intercepted by a nurse who had been looking after the waning surrealist. She'd heard I was at Ronnie's (it must have been almost December, but I recall a fine day – how ageing memory plays tricks!), and she wondered if I could get her boyfriend free tickets. Aware of how badly hospital staff were paid and that anyway she was ministering to my old and valiant friend, I agreed and did so, leaving the tickets at the desk and warning the staff.

They came all right and showed up in our break. She told me in a stage whisper that her boyfriend was an alcoholic, a fact self-evident to the naked eye and, if he staggered close enough, the nose. I immediately named her Nurse Pot and he Mr Kettle. Eventually they reeled back to their table, but shortly afterwards one of the door staff appeared and told me that they were making such a noise and annoying so many people that he'd come to ask me if I minded if he got rid of them.

I explained how they had come to be my guests and, feeling only minimally like St Peter, gave him full permission to throw them into Frith Street. I never heard from Nurse Pot again.

That was '04. Early in '05, and on the same night, Digby and I suffered from equal monsters. I was first. A 35-ish-looking man with a bald head and glasses, and slightly but not apparently very drunk, came up to me and flourished a twenty-pound note under my nose. 'I want you to sign that,' he said, 'and then we'll drink a double whiskey together.' I told him 'no' on both counts. To sign a banknote, if you weren't the President of the Bank of England, was absurd. 'I'll never spend it,' he assured me. 'I never would.' I doubted his word on the grounds that eventually he'd find himself without funds and a necessity to pay for something. He continued to deny he ever would spend it. Ever!

I suggested that he use it to buy a CD or a book. He refused and returned to try to persuade me. I was getting a little, no, a lot irritated. He eventually let the question of the note drop and proposed we drink his double whiskeys. I refused that too, on the grounds that during a performance I watched my intake and had fulfilled it. He wouldn't have it. Over and over he pushed the note at me and proposed the whiskey. Up until then he had been leaning on the table. Now he came round it and sat between Digby and me. Finally I did something I very rarely do. I lost my temper, an event which is usually so unexpected and unconvincing that those present are forced to 'corpse', as they say on the stage, or suppress their laughter.

I turned to my tormentor. 'You are without doubt,' I told him with the calm that precedes a tropical storm, 'the most boring man I have ever met.' I paused while he took this in, and then yelled at the top of my voice (the palm trees bent double, corrugated-iron roofs and coconuts flew through the air, great waves crashed against the shore), 'FUCK OFF!' Even this had only a delayed impact, but, after several repetitions, he went.

Digby's experience later that same evening was even more dramatic.

We were still in the downstairs bar, still selling and signing, when I had to go for a pee. During my absence (it often takes me some time these days because, although it seems urgent, I have to whistle to get it going) a weasel-faced man came and sat by Digby and asked him if it wouldn't be possible on my return to con some money out of me. It's true that many people imagine because I'm quite well known that I am also rich. They're wrong. I'm a spender, not a saver. I love, when I have money, going to expensive restaurants and taking taxis. In general though, to use a memorable phrase of somebody's invention, I would describe myself as 'broke but not poor'.

Even so, had I been Croesus, or Midas or all the Rothschilds, Digby, my true friend after all, would have been furious. I knew he had depths below his surface ebullient charm, but to see the rage break the surface of his general bonhomie like a furious sea-monster emerging from six miles down was an awe-inspiring moment.

'FUCK OFF!' he shouted at weasel-face and, rising and repeating this simple injunction at ever-louder volume, he assumed, when they reached the bar, the posture of a Regency bare-knuckle boxer. The weasel was beginning to look extremely nervous.

I had returned from the gents at this point and was very impressed, if, as yet, unaware of the cause of the furore.

Digby continued, still holding his 1820-ish pose. 'If you don't FUCK OFF,' he reiterated, 'I'll send for Pete King,' a gentleman of whom weasel I doubt had ever heard, but must have imagined as a composite of Frank Bruno and Reggie Kray. 'And he,' snarled Digby, 'will send for the door staff and throw you into the street without any hesitation. So FUCK OFF!' But by this time weasel-face was already half-way up the stairs.

Digby and I discussed this double whammy later and had to admit we had both enjoyed this flood of adrenalin. Yes, really enjoyed it!

No such disturbance for the rest of the run and the taxi still worked its magic as I climbed into it under the swinging red neon saxophone above the double doors.

9. Ronnie

The right of man to his own suicide –
Surrealist pamphlet

In a book like this it seems fitting that I should write a few friendly obituaries of people I have admired and who, although they may have 'left the building', continue to influence me. Since I've written about his club, I should begin with Ronnie Scott.

Ronnie, like a large number of modernist musicians, was of Jewish East End origin. He didn't appear to me either to exploit or conceal this. He reminded me of a sketch in *Beyond the Fringe*, where Jonathan Miller stands alone while the other three talk about him as a Jew. Eventually Miller is irritated enough to react. 'I'm not a Jew!' he snaps at them. 'I'm Jewish.' This, in my view, applied to Ronnie. He only once made a Jewish joke in my hearing. He described the ultimate proof of ecumenical progress as a 'ham-bagel'.

I only once saw him at all irascible in a Jewish context. It was the wedding of his friend the late Benny Green, in a North London synagogue. It was an entirely traditional ceremony: the canopy, the smashing of the symbolic plate, Hebrew and a proper rabbi with a beard. Ronnie was standing next to me and said nothing until the chanting started. This so irritated him that he hissed in my ear, 'I don't know how long it is since I went to schul, but they're fucking up the traditional harmonies. They've *Westernized* them.' I felt, though, that he was scandalized not as a Jew but as a musician.

I don't intend to go in any detail into Ronnie's early years and their musical history: his influences, his first trips to America, his fight to establish a public for bop. All I need say is that for us revivalists, or 'Mouldie Fygges', as the bop musicians contemptuously called us, he was simply 'the enemy', the Napoleon of the flattened fifth.

In the 1950s my agent at that time, Jim Godbolt, and myself, both convinced revivalists (although Jim, within that fairly wide field, had a greater enthusiasm for early white jazz than I) assumed imaginary cloaks, wide-brimmed hats and dark glasses and visited Club Eleven, arguably the first bop stronghold in London. It was, in retrospect, a sensational gathering of modern musicians: not only Ronnie but also Tony Crombie, Lennie Bush and Johnnie Dankworth. George Robey, 'the Prime Minister of Mirth', used to recite a monologue accompanied at the piano which my mother would often quote on what she felt were appropriate occasions. The last line went: 'So I stopped, and I looked – and I left!' Jim and I likewise. We went into a nearby pub in Soho and snorted like two old colonels over our half pints. Little could we have guessed that two decades later Jim would be editing the Scott club's monthly magazine and I would be appearing there for over thirty years on the trot.

In the interim I got to know Ronnie and several other major figures in the bop world such as the late Tubby Hayes, and found them witty human beings and not the perverse ear-smashers and leg-pullers we had imagined. More, not only did Humph swim into the mainstream but several erstwhile 'Mouldie Fygges' became converted to bop itself. Keith Christie, the best revivalist trombonist Lyttelton ever employed, was one such. Dickie Hawdon, originally on trumpet in the ultra-revivalist Yorkshire Jazz Band, was another. There was also Dill Janes, pianist and Welsh charmer, who could play and was equally enthusiastic in every idiom from Jelly Roll Morton to Thelonius Monk; while for some years, as hopeless as a peace-maker in the Middle East, he at least could talk to both schools. I went at some point to his flat for a party of bop musicians and their cool svelte girlfriends. There, for the first time, I smelt the pungent and pleasant fumes of marijuana.

So, at least by the time we moved into Ronnie's, we were less apprehensive than we might have been, and anyway John Chilton, with his love for small Harlem swing bands of the thirties, had less far to move.

Ronnie himself, while no matinée idol, was attractive in a thin, hidden-depths way and turned out to be more complex than I had imagined. I knew him as a formidable comic, cynical, hard-edged, and with a sense of timing the equal of any musical star past or present, but I hadn't realized that, like many on 'the Halls', he suffered from acute bouts of depression.

He always played the interval spots at the club during our season, so I got to hear him a great deal. His early influences had been digested, his style was tough and sinuous, but you could tell that musically he was entirely serious. I admired what I'd now call, however contradictorily, the hard-edged fluidity of his music. At times, many stars of stage, screen and radio, not to say politicians from every party, came in, but Ronnie never allowed this to shake him. The MD at that time was, while friendly and helpful, something of a star-fucker. Very over-excited, he ran into the office behind the stage where Ronnie was warming up.

'Liza Minnelli's out front,' he announced as breathlessly as if bringing news of a successful medieval battle to his monarch.

Ronnie, the master of cool, said, 'Oh yes. Well I've got things to blow,' and, raising his sax again, continued to rehearse runs and cadenzas.

I, however, am almost as much of a star-fucker as the MD (if, I hope, less obviously), and during our interval was very pleased to join Liza Minnelli, at her request, for a drink. She batted her long eyelashes at me and said, 'Momma would have *loved* your numbers!' Could she have told me anything more calculated to please?

If, while admiring his dedication, I was never a complete convert to Ronnie's 'organic' bop, his humour was a different matter. Every night he was appearing he would stroll on and tell clusters of jokes on various topics. This routine, all thirty or so minutes of it, was always the same. Yet, in the same way that I could listen with total pleasure to the set routine of Max Miller, I loved it. Timing in comedy is more important than content. I did once ask Ronnie why, since he was a spontaneously witty man, he didn't change any of his jokes. 'Oh they do change,' he said. And then, after a pause, added, 'imperceptibly'.

As dear Ronnie 'left the building' eight years ago (at the time of writing) and increasingly in the future there will be fewer and fewer people who actually heard him live, here are some of his 'imperceptibly' changing gags.

General jokes
Of the staff:
'That waitress – she just moved! Mind you, she's a very intelligent girl. I asked her if she liked Dickens. She told me she'd never been to one. She thinks Moby Dick's a venereal disease. She eats a banana sideways.'

Of a very fat man who at one time worked on the door: 'Then there's Big Henry. His shadow weighs more than I do. He eats furniture for lunch.'

'The chef here is very good. Pygmies come all the way from Africa to dip their arrows in his soup.' And then, after a thoughtful pause and sotto voce, 'How do you fuck up cornflakes?'

On mentioning a musician due to appear in the near future: 'He's the best in the country. Mind you, in the town he's lousy.'

Of the club:
'This club always reminds me of home. It's filthy and full of strangers!'

For some reason the East Coast resort of Scunthorpe, where most touring bands had played over the years, inspired Ronnie into inventing a series of observations which could hardly have delighted the town's publicity officer. An example: 'My bedroom was so small, every time I opened the door the handle rearranged the furniture.'

Defensive ploys

If there was not much reaction to any of his jokes, he would tap his hand-held mike and enquire anxiously, 'Is this thing working?'

If no attention at all was being paid, he would stare at the party seated nearest the stage and ask himself, 'Why do I always get a table of dead Greeks?'

A mere sample, but I hope you will grasp the flavour.

As he left the stage, inevitably he would round off his act with the laconic sign-off: 'So much for humour.'

Ronnie's occasional periods of depression seemed to be brought on most often by the departure of his current and always beautiful girlfriend. Why they left him was, to me at any rate, a mystery. Could it have been they felt that he loved his sax and the club itself more than them, with his worldwide tours an additional cause? This is pure speculation on my part but, when they did leave, they hid, not in London or even in the provinces, but in the far-flung corners of the earth – New Zealand, perhaps, or Canada. When he found out where they'd gone, he would follow them to try, in each case unsuccessfully, to persuade them to come back. Their refusal was the camel's straw. It brought on a breakdown, sometimes leading to a period in a nursing-home.

I went to see him on one of these sad occasions. He was almost silent, and it was like visiting a zombie. But then he would recover, another beauty would fall under his irresistible spell, he'd blow again with renewed passion, and the table of dead Greeks, the pygmies, Scunthorpe and Moby Dick were resurrected.

The year of his death, however, there were many additional reasons for his despair, although the absconding of his latest *belle-de-nuit* was certainly contributory. They were: his teeth, as essential to a horn-player as hands are to a pianist, were causing him great pain and his hope to have new ones embedded was impossible, his dentist told him, because his gums were too weak. He was about to be seventy, a birthday he dreaded. And he hated Christmas (snap). Not a bad list for a depressive.

Actually John Chilton had observed several changes that season. Usually Ronnie opened the door to the dressing-room when it was time for us to go on stage and said one word, 'Gentlemen'. But this time he came and sat with us most evenings and talked about the past. Once, when we were having a private conversation, he confided that he felt that, musically, he'd said all he had to say.

On the last night I saw him alive he did something unprecedented: he went on stage to tell his jokes and the audience, many of them drunken office partiers or noisy yuppies and their bimbos round the bar, were, as was usual during that season, shouting at each other at full volume. Usually, irritated or not, he just ploughed ahead, but this time, not long after he'd started, he stopped and told them, 'If you don't want to hear my jokes I'm fucked if I want to tell them!' and stalked off.

That Christmas, too, his only daughter had come over from the States to keep him company, although I got the impression that their relationship was not all that easy. On the night he died they'd had a ferocious row in his Chelsea flat, and she'd left to go home. He rang her up and pleaded with her to come back, but, given how unpleasant he'd been, she refused, thinking she would return to make it up next morning. She did, but found him dead on the floor by his bed. There was an empty bottle of pills and a bottle of vodka on the carpet.

Suicide? Many people, including myself, thought so. Others believed that it was an accidental overdose. As far as I could see, though, the press never printed or even hinted at my former conclusion.

The police informed Pete King, his long-time business partner and best friend, first, and he, while clearly deeply upset, told us that evening, but asked us not to let it out to the full house until the end of our second set. It had already reached the staff, however, and they were all crying, which didn't make our 'show must go on' endeavours any easier. After our last number, 'Nuts', as far as I can remember, I told the audience and they were completely silent. The next day the press reported it, but their reaction was a complete surprise. Front-page headlines in almost every case, and all favourable, either on the page or in the editorial comments. What's more, when later there was a memorial service at St Martin's-in-the-Fields, Trafalgar Square (a strange place to commemorate a nice Jewish boy), not only was the church full to capacity (no need for the vergers to 'throw them in off the streets') but there was a huge crowd outside. The other media, TV and radio, also mourned the lonely death of a bop saxophonist. Only the death of Princess Diana attracted such attention – but Ronnie's was without the flowers or the hysteria.

From then on, on a large table in the lobby of the club there has always been a vase holding a beautiful bunch of fresh flowers in Ronnie's memory. On the walls throughout the whole premises are photographs of him and in the downstairs bar a semi-cubist portrait. Sometimes he is alone, sometimes with the many jazz stars, both British and American, who have appeared there. His wry spirit haunts the building and especially the stage, where he blew his heart out night after night. We remember Ronnie all right.

Not so long ago (this is March '05) I was asked by the *Evening Standard* to write a piece on 'Is Jazz Dead?', a question frequently posed over the years when they need to fill a features page. It was to find out my reaction to the news that Jazz FM was about to change its name to Smooth FM. It was, I felt, not before time. Despite Jazz FM's brave beginnings, its name had long become inappropriate. Jazz proper was by then confined to about an hour on Sunday night; the rest, at best cocktail bar music, was meant to soothe housewives at their repetitive tasks, and for them even the word 'jazz' was off-putting, too challenging, and besides what was 'jazz' anyway? Not much to do with cleaning the oven, making beds or wiping the baby's bum, and appealing only to a comparatively small public. And so, in order to increase the listening figures, jazz was a word to drop, which the station eventually did.

But to cheer up the piece I concluded with an optimistic reflection. Ronnie Scott's club had grown from its tentative beginnings in a grimy basement, to become the most respected jazz venue in the world, the place where it was considered an honour to be booked.

Yet it was always threatened by economic difficulties. Some artistes, who demanded and deserved a huge fee, could pack it for weeks at a time. Others, especially if at all experimental, drew a very limited audience. On top of that, premises in Soho became more and more expensive. Rents and rates soared, closing many much-loved small family businesses, most of them of Italian or French origin, which had given the district its attractive village atmosphere. Cheap restaurants and cafés were, with very few exceptions, taken over by expensive chains; the whores were banished from the streets to become call-girls, mostly owned and exploited by pimps; sex shops, at least much reduced these days by their need to hold a licence, seemed to me depressing, with their multi-sized dildos and blow-up sex dolls. Only a few clubs remain from my youth. Indeed, ex-con turned author Frank Norman wrote a musical about this change. He called it 'Fings Ain't Wot They Used T' Be'.

And Ronnie's? Difficult to manoeuvre in order to keep up with vastly increased upkeep. At intervals it seemed near to collapse, but Ronnie's name and presence and Pete King's refusal to give in to market forces saved it, usually 'in the nick of time', as they used to write in curly letters on a black ground to punctuate those exciting weekly serials of the silent screen. On several occasions, too, someone, a rich jazz lover or benevolent or guilty capitalist, would take up the burden, placate the bank, and Ronnie's was saved.

But only temporarily. Sooner or later, the current Mycenae, alarmed by his rapidly shrinking bank account, bowed out, but then, as Ronnie used to say, 'the only way to make a million out of jazz is to invest two million.'

This time, however, the benefactor seems much more solid and permanent: a lady called Sally Green (a name that could well form the opening words of one of those mildly indecent vaudeville songs of the twenties: 'Miss Sally Green

'The only way to make a million out of jazz is to invest two million'

of New Orleans/She ran a buffet flat' – 'Soft Pedalling Blues', Bessie Smith) who is married to an American millionaire with a deep love and knowledge of jazz, and the personal friendship of everyone in the world who loves the music, ex-President Clinton (sax) among others.

Furthermore she has met and got on well with Pete, and intends to do something about the cuisine, although I hope somebody warns the pygmies in good time to stay where they are in the rainforest. She sounds a five-star lady and I wrote about her in the *Standard* as the antidote to 'Smooth FM' ('Bland' would have been even more apt, but perhaps over the top).

Then I got a very hurt phone call from Pete. It also didn't make much sense. He said I'd suggested that the club's difficulties had begun only after Ronnie's death. I never did or would. That the welcome intervention of Ms Green was meant to be a secret and I'd blown it, and that he had thought of me as a real friend. I assured him that I too would always think of him very warmly, but that as to Ms Green's identity, it had been sprung in a long article about her in the *Daily Telegraph* only a few days earlier, so was surely not hush-hush. His reaction to that was 'That was another drag', which doesn't make much sense in context, but I do know how much he loved and misses Ronnie, how sensitive he is about him. I rang him a few days later and we got on fine. He said, which I certainly suspected, that whereas Ronnie hadn't played much part in running the business he was, as Pete rather touchingly put it, 'a shoulder to cry on'. Also they had been together for so many years, fought for what they believed in musically (Pete King had originally played sax himself but recognized his talent was more administrative than musical and assumed his present role), faced triumph and near-disaster, and now of course that partnership was all over. He nearly reduced me to tears.

A mystery, however, remains. Bop is now accepted jazz history, but not a widely popular music. Its true public, while convinced of the pleasure to be derived from it, its importance in the history of jazz and its value as art, is still, though much larger than it was, a minority. Most people over, say, twenty know of the club's existence, and many have been there and heard Ronnie blow his uncompromising horn, but this cannot explain the outburst of grief at his death, the crowds inside and outside the church only half a mile from the club itself.

My feeling is that he possessed what the Catholics believe to be a mysterious glow surrounding their saints – charisma. Of the many artists in both jazz and rock, a mere handful are still universally mourned: I can cite John Lennon, Charlie Parker, Elvis Presley, Jimi Hendrix, Billie Holiday. There are many more we admire and miss but that is on a different level.

Ronnie once asked me what benefits were to be expected from his MBE. Money? 'No,' I said. 'A better table in posh restaurants?' 'No, you'd get that from being Ronnie Scott.' 'Upgrading on planes?' 'Same difference.' And I concluded, 'It won't impress your bookmaker either!' At this he allowed himself a wry smile. 'So,' he said, 'it's no use at all!' I suspect, however, that, like most people, he was flattered to have received it.

So how did Ronnie Scott MBE, this obsessive gambler, East End Jewish saxophonist, one-time gaol-bird for possessing a small amount of pot back in the draconian and hysterical post-war period, this acute manic-depressive, have the power to demand our love, to make us feel loss? We shall not look upon (or hear) his like again.

And a big bear-hug from me for Pete King OBE.

10. Discomforts and Pleasures

It is early in 2005, and generally, I am well. Dr Watson, while of course still disapproving of my intake of drink and my renewed smoking, was pleased with my chest, no wheezing, but felt I needed some iron pills. At the hospital the specialist said my calcium count was still up, but not so bad as to necessitate surgical treatment. What I ate didn't matter; I noticed the other day some yogurt I was spooning down claimed to be 'full of calcium', but he said that didn't matter either. The villain, it seems, is a small gland near the throat working overtime, but yes, an operation could affect my singing. Bugger that!

I'm walking much better but if, as sometimes happens, my right knee seizes up I have to go up and down a staircase sideways, although an application of Olbas Oil, a natural product brought to my thankful attention by my homeopathic-minded brother-in-law, soon eases it and indeed all other aches and pains.

I sleep a great deal. I probably would anyway, as my nights are made restless due to my pee pills, at least eight visits to the loo six feet from my bed and lasting up to 6 a.m. But then all my contemporaries take siestas and none of them suffers from water retention. We all rhapsodize about the joy of climbing into bed. It's almost erotic.

The only place my back and ankles play me up is at art galleries, especially annoying as there are several wonderful exhibitions I haven't *yet* seen. Fortunately most public galleries have benches at fairly frequent intervals where I can slump and straighten my back, a trick I learnt when fishing for too long in middle age. I've tried a wheelchair but that needs someone to push it and Venetia, with whom I used to attend many shows, likes to move at her own pace, not mine, and is embarrassed, not to say irritated, by my tendency to express my views in a loud voice as a result of my deafness.

I am also conducting a series of visits to my sweet dentist, Dr Couttino, a woman of Eastern origin whose many brothers are all doctors of one sort or another. A few days ago she gave me three local injections, each accompanied by a loud squeak as the needle went in. What she was up to was removing the root of a cap which had broken off. Of course it didn't hurt, as my upper jaw was completely numb after twenty minutes reading *Hello* magazine in the waiting-room while the injection hit. But it was quite noisy, as she used a kind of minute electric screwdriver to loosen the cap. She told me (Brr! Brr!) that she worked slowly for fear of chipping the root further, but her assistant gave me a pair of very dirty spectacles. Thinking they belonged to her I pointed this out but, explained Dr Couttino, they belonged to nobody. She just asked me to wear them to protect my eyes in case a fragment of tooth flew into the eyeball.

At last the root came away and she held it up for me to see. It was quite large and like a modern sculpture carved from red coral. The red was my blood which, despite various cotton or cloth plugs, took a long time to staunch. This achieved, she told me I could eat, or drink (or smoke, I thought) anything as long as it was not too hot. The fragment that was once me went into the pedal bin.

Next week I go back for the extraction of another root on the other side of my mouth. Then the two missing teeth are to be added to my top plate, and there are quite a number of small fillings to attend to later. She did tell me, however, that I was brushing my teeth and gums much more thoroughly. A small bring-up.

Her surgery is part of a practice. It's in the sub-basement in one of the anonymous terraces leading off Exhibition Road and faces a small park. The function of the rest of the building is unknown to me though it is probably connected with a branch of Imperial College.

There is, happily, a modern lift, metal-lined and with a feature I have always, perhaps childishly, found pleasing: you enter the lift facing the ground floor, but exit through another door opening at the side, like a secret panel.

I used to attend private dentists in Harley Street when the fees were still comparatively modest and anyway I was earning a great deal more. There was always a large waiting-room full of intimidating, heavy and gloomy furniture inlaid with brass, with only current posh magazines, *Country Life* and its companions, laid out neatly on a large polished table. Today my National Health equivalent is bright and unthreatening. The secretaries are welcoming and efficient, although when I first went there a strange, very old lady paced and mumbled her way around behind the desk. I supposed her continued presence was due to the charity of her employers, or perhaps she needed her salary. Both reasons seemed equally admirable. Anyway she is long gone.

The waiting-room itself, straight on past the desk, is fairly narrow and faces the three surgery doors. The chairs are comfortable and well designed in wood and aluminium and there are some with faintly sinister goo-goo eyes below the seat for nervous children. The magazines are in various states of disintegration.

Leaving Dr Couttino's yesterday I aimed for a small super-market adjoining a café which has a bar in the basement, almost salivating at the thought of a large G with ice and lemon and the mouth-watering clink as the tonic hits the ice. There was also a packet of unopened Marlboro Lites and a lighter in my sweater's zip-up pocket.

IT WAS SHUT FOR THE EASTER WEEKEND.

After a few moments, like Beatrix Potter's two bad mice, of 'rage and disappointment', I made off instead for a pub in nearby Kensington. En route I passed the V & A Museum. What an area this is for deification of Prince Albert! Not only the V & A itself, not only Exhibition Road, but the memorial, recently cleaned and re-gilded, and facing it the Albert Hall itself – all concrete proof of the profound grief of the Widow of Windsor.

The pub itself, the Hoop and Toy, is small and its exterior late nineteenth-century baroque. Its interior is cosy. It played a slight and mildly ludicrous role in my past. In the fifties, in circumstances which now escape me, perhaps a gig in what was then the nearby Royal College of Art, I found myself with Mick Mulligan, my band-leader, and his clari-nettist, Ian Christie, at the bar there. We had such a good time that we made one of those optimistic, alcohol-inspired decisions to meet there every week! Of course none of us ever did, not once, and it became a band joke, but here I was again, in my seventies, gulping and puffing away at a table. The only drawback to the place is that, in common with most old pubs and many theatres too, the gents is down a steep flight of steps.

I went home, not all that far after all, in a taxi, although nowadays, if convenient (no changes and the like) and I'm feeling especially spry, I take one of the big red buses or a tube.

Next morning Shirley, my secretary, came. When I mentioned my dental visit, she told me she too had a root extracted on the same day and her dentist had given her exactly the same instructions: no rinsing, any food or drink but nothing too hot. The only difference, due either to Dr Couttino's superior skill or, more likely, my tougher nervous system, was that she'd suffered considerable pain when the injection had worn off. Smug me. I felt none, I told her, although the gap is still just a shade tender and I chew food on the other side of my mouth.

Unless there's a crisis, this, I promise you, is the last medical report until in a week or so I have a scan before visiting Dr Kohn for a check-up on my lungs.

After this reassuring but minimal description of my very 'slight discomfort' I feel I should balance things by listing what I suppose I should call my 'minimal pleasures'.

First, I suppose, I'd put fishing top of the list. Although much curtailed, it's still an activity which I shall never entirely abandon if I can help it. At the beginning of this still-teething century I published a book called *Hooked* which was concerned with the 'why' rather than the 'how' of angling. It finished just after we'd sold the Tower (Norman in origin) on the great and improving River Usk, where I'd cast for twenty years, and bought a cottage in Bagnor, near Newbury,

Berkshire. It's a charming village and faces, across a jungle of pretty weeds, a narrow tributary of the Lambourne, which is a chalk stream with many trout, some large, and has benches for the benefit of old gents to sit and remember their days pig-sticking in India or sending murderers to the gallows.

The village is about a mile away or more, despite the current improvement in what Fats Waller called his 'pedal extremities'; this means transport. Diana, having defeated the possibility of my being carried back to the Tower lifeless on a barn door, was aware I had become too wobbly to resume mounting a moped and being brought home to the cottage on a billboard advertising the next race meeting at Newbury race-track. She came up with a practical idea – a granny-mobile! Of course this is not what they're really called. Mine, insofar as I can remember, is named very inappropriately the 'eagle', or some other member of the animal kingdom noted for its ability to put on bursts of incredible speed, hardly appropriate for the old ladies (less often gents for some reason) doing their shopping in the supermarket on such machines. Animals, though, seem to be an obsession of the manufacturers. There is, on mine, a knob with an arrow, backed up by a switch, which can make you go faster or slower. If you turn the arrow to the left until it's pointing at the image of a tortoise, the vehicle can't go more than four miles an hour – rather faster than the average tortoise, I'd have thought. But even more question- able is that if you turn the knob to the right there is the image of a hare. Going downhill you can get up to about six miles an hour top whack but I don't think the average hare pursued by a predator, swerve as it may, would last very long at that pace. If you've been driving slowly though, and then change pace suddenly, it does give the illusion of competing in a Grand Prix.

As a technology dunce (I call myself the Ned Ludd of the computer), I must say the machine is almost absurdly simple to master. You insert a black bayonet key big enough to be difficult to lose into a hole in the side of the anti-dashboard, press the lever on the left and you go backwards, press the right and you move forwards. Release both and it stops. There is also a switch activating both the front and back lights at the same time and another switch to flick them on and off to show you've pulled up or are in trouble, a horn button producing a noise not loud enough to excite Mr Toad and two other buttons on the opposite ends of the dashboard to indicate I'm going left (the left-hand button) or right (guess).

That's about all. Fuel? Under a flap at the back end is a length of black electric cable, coiled like a snake with a conventional plug at one end. When you get home you just plug it in and turn it on. In the morning it's fully charged. How can you tell? There is a panel centred right in front of your nose with an indicator in bands of different colours: dark green, raring to go like a greyhound in the traps, paler green, via yellow (remember to recharge it later) to dark orange (keep your fingers crossed).

I hope I haven't bored the leathers off you with this detailed description of my much-loved machine. It's my revenge for those macho car-owning figures who have bent my unreceptive ear mercilessly, despite my protesting I'm in no way interested in what they tend to call 'me motor'.

There are still a few outside features to go. There is a

small wire basket at the front for purchases ('Look, Albert, I've remembered your Bengers') and at the side, low down behind the saddle, a deeper metal basket intended for your crutches. When I'm going fishing I put my rod in there (the front basket holds my net, fishing bag and eventually, if I've had a successful day, trout). People used to ask me, on seeing my extended rod, 'Why have you got an aerial on your machine?' Actually, of late I've taken to breaking down my rod because the tip has twice snapped off when it caught the lower branches of a tree.

While a figure of fun to passing youngsters, the machine can be driven on the pavement (the tortoise in evidence), up one-way streets and parked more or less at random. There is, it seems, no road tax, although I'm not sure about insurance – but anyway it's no great financial burden.

Incidentally, for those who are royal snobs, the late Queen Mother waved to people from one in her final years in the streets around St James's Palace on her birthday. In her case, however, there was a uniformed chauffeur by her side. Even if I could afford it, I couldn't follow her lead there. My granny-mobile holds only one. A pity, because I could easily imitate the languid wave patented by the House of Windsor (wave, wave, smile a bit – but not too much! – wave, wave).

Actually, out of that entire family I had some empathy for the Queen Mum. It seems she drank too much, loved the company of queens and overspent wildly, three vices I share. I hear too that during the Blitz she spent quite a lot of time secretly in the Lake District where someone spotted her by chance and was sworn to secrecy by her minders. I don't hold this against her. Why did she have to remain in Buck House all the time, a sitting target for a German airman?

Anyway, she did visit the East End with her shy, stammering husband. Someone sent me quite a long list of what East Enders are purported to have said about her strolls through Hackney or the dock areas. I don't know, of course, how truthful this anthology of favourable reactions is, but my favourite quote is this. A woman, after meeting her: 'She said, "They tell lies about you. You don't smell of shit."'

She too, in her younger days, was an angler. When fishing for salmon on a Scottish river, she was spotted by a woman casting from the other shore, who concluded she was poaching. Wading into mid-stream, she recognized 'the poacher' and performed a low curtsy, her thigh waders filled up with water and she was swept downstream by the current, but, happily, not fatally.

Finally, something connected with her which I witnessed myself. My father took me to the Grand National at Aintree and we stood near the winning post. The Queen Mother, like her daughter, had a keen interest in racing and her horse (you can imagine the excitement in the Royal Enclosure) was streaking ahead, well in front of the field. Within a few yards of the post, all its legs splayed and it collapsed. A woman standing next to us was desperately upset and, in a strong Liverpool accent, burst out with, 'Surely they'll let it win, won't they?'

So, one way or another, I was more pro than anti the boozing, overspending homophile – but, apart from the Queen who performs her boring duties in a suitably boring way, I am appalled by the rest of the House of Dyslexia, some pathetic, some arrogant. Here's to your memory, Queen Mum. And if your chauffeur is driving your granny-mobile up the celestial glens, unscrew the top of your stick (which they say contained a hollow flask of gin and dry Martini) and knock it back.

Much as my doctor disapproves – she called me incorrigible on my last visit – I too still drink, most of the time Irish whiskey, mostly of an evening and especially at the conclusions of gigs, particularly if the band and I patronize the hotel bar. If I haven't eaten before the concert (it depends on the time available between the sound-check and the first number), it's usually a small Italian restaurant (I love those huge phallic pepper grinders), Chinese or Indian. If Italian, I usually settle for spaghetti bolognese. I prefer the long variety wound round a fork held against a spoon (dead common, so Andrée's posh Italian communist friends told her: the *bottom* of the plate should act as the fulcrum). I also tuck in my napkin to save spillage down my shirt, tie and lapels. (I'm usually wearing my band suit by this time.) Most people, if I'm dining *à deux*, find it vaguely embarrassing. My excuse, uttered like a ritual, is, 'Like a Belgian senator'. I don't know, in fact, if Belgian senators do this at all, nor where the phrase comes from.

This position saves me constantly grovelling under the table to retrieve my elusive napkin which immediately slips to the floor if spread across my knees. Is it my shape? I feel it's akin to my inability (no hips and small buttocks), even when my stomach was enormous – my great and long-time friend the painter Maggi Hambling claimed that my gut, which she loved, entered the room long before I did – to keep my trousers up without clip-on braces.

I'm quite thin now, which just happened recently. I didn't resort to nibbling a single lettuce leaf washed down with

Brecon water like a supermodel. On the other hand, I do eat much less, quite often only one meal a day, and if I order something substantial even then I often can't finish it ('Delicious, but I've a very small appetite'). I can, however, always manage a pudding, having like many old people developed a sweet tooth. Still, my jowls have vanished, replaced by modified turkey-like wattles. Looking at photographs taken only a couple of years back, I see I was quite neckless and my face was almost circular like a child's drawing of the sun. In fact, people who haven't seen me for some time tend to say, 'You *have* lost weight' in that mildly worried tone of voice that suggests I'm about to tell them some bad, perhaps fatal, physical news. I reassure them, and relieved they add, 'You are looking well, though,' misinterpreting my whiskey flush as the reward for early nights, a sensible gastronomic regime and lots of fresh air.

Some of my favourite foods are denied me. For example, I had a bad oyster years ago. When I tried some again recently, they had a disastrous effect. The ageing stomach seems to have developed an elephantine memory and, however long the gap, reacts instantly. The same is even more the case if I gobble down *moules marinières*, an old favourite of mine. Other foods may be harmless in themselves, but if they coincide with a bad attack of the trots, I cross them off my OK list. Bacon for one, and I love it, especially when crisp in the American manner, although cooked like that it can splinter and jump, justifying the Belgian senator's precaution.

I have developed fairly recently an almost pregnant woman-like passion for bananas. They do me no harm and have a unique flavour, if correctly ripe. My obsessive love of neatness is satisfied by the way they are so neatly contained within their skin (only the egg is their rival here).

Citrus fruits, tomatoes and especially strawberries are forbidden as provokers of arthritis. I sometimes, guiltily and in a very restrained way, break this taboo, especially in the case of fried tomatoes, preferably on fried bread, part of every Thursday's cooked breakfast in my childhood, although the fried bread tends, like American-style bacon, to bombard my Belgian senator's apron.

That's about all to report, except the big-toe nails which during my psoriasis days were pushed out of shape and discoloured. Whereas I can clip (just) the smaller nails, especially when the outside ones start to catch my socks, the big ones need the chiropodist with her astounding collection of scissors, which look like a medieval dwarf's instruments of torture.

That's quite enough, probably far too much, about my current health and needs. Don't, by the way, put any of this reporting down to physical vanity. I'm long past that and today, peering into the enlarging side of the shaving mirror, I agree wholeheartedly with what my mother used to repeat constantly in her last decade, 'You can't tell me that old age is pretty!' Too true, Maudie!

Restaurants remain a pleasure, but today a much more occasional one. They come under my list of 'treats'. My friend Venetia thinks of them as a 'celebration' and expects everyone rich and fond of her (or even not so rich) to demonstrate their fondness by the simple, if increasingly expensive gesture of taking her for a meal.

Now she has a title (her late husband was a viscount). I

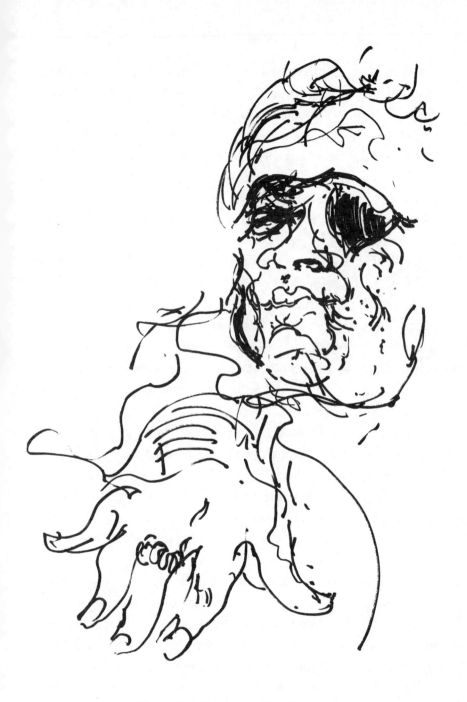

'You can't tell me that old age is pretty!'

always mention this when booking on the telephone. Head waiters and managers love it. ''Er Ledysheep 'as arrivée', they tell me if she's early or I'm late.

Jim Godbolt, an old friend, past agent and sparring partner of mine, has many prejudices, among them a hatred of public schools and a suspicion of all those who were educated (or mis-educated) there. He also detests the idea of chic restaurants. So to tease him I sometimes say, 'I must rush because . . .'

'A little dinner, is it, George?' he asks. 'All the flim-flam of West End eating?'

Well, if by flim-flam he means good service and delicious food – yes. But in fact I also enjoy the ritual of it, almost religious at times, and Venetia's gossip about many of the other diners which would be thoroughly enjoyable if I could still hear her. As it is, if I ask her to repeat it, she hisses at me in exasperation, 'I can't shout.'

My Uncle Fred took me, as a child in Liverpool, to the State Grill Room for what I thought he called 'Chicken on the gorilla', which amused him. I, exploitative little sod that I was, also asked for 'suggestive biscuits'. 'Isn't he sweet?' grown-ups would coo.

The State's interior décor was amazing. Arts and crafts I've always supposed, but in its late and decadent period: huge medallions on the walls throughout, mostly sea-faring in subject, but seeming modelled in wax and then heavily varnished. The rest all fitted in: heavy silver cutlery, gleaming glass, big napkins (this was, however, long before the Belgian senator was helped into his chair) and ornate plates.

They greeted my Uncle Fred warmly, who obviously took his business clients there, and I was impressed by that too.

Strangely enough, some time in the seventies or eighties, John Chilton and I played the State, temporarily a jazz club. It seemed in no way changed, although 'the Gorilla' was extinguished and Uncle Fred too.

In the lobby stood a very pretty be-jeaned blonde with that faint accent typical of Liverpool suburban girls. Immediately, she made it quite clear that she fancied me. Despite some wavering at the end of our second set, we eventually went back in a taxi to her place, a small, chaotic bedsit. The truth of 'the certainty of hazard' was at work again in that it was round the corner from the pub where my father used to drink with his circle and the street where my mother and, come to that, her mother, used to shop.

In my new friend's messy room were posters of rock stars and local footballers and a number of cuddly animals. She told me her boyfriend was out of town for some weeks and that she worked in the office of a big firm in the city centre. As we drank our Nescafé she added that at a fixed time, both morning and afternoon, she went for 'a ciggy and a wank in the office lavy'. Mulligan called this sort of revelation 'hot chat' and its effect here was to guarantee me a very horny night, all the more so because it was bang in the middle of an area buttered with memories of my childhood and adolescence.

In the morning, after she'd gone to work ('Christ, I'll be late for werk!'), I, though knowing it to be absurd, couldn't resist tidying everything up. (Venetia used to be driven mad by my tidying. She is an untidy woman, and she took to calling me 'Winnie' and pretending I was her Edwardian lady's maid.) I made Carole's bed (a possible Turner Prize entry), sorted out the LPs and rock mags and let myself out.

I found myself immediately in Lark Lane and began to walk towards Aigburth Road to catch a bus (how I regret the passing of the tram, or 'car', as it was known) to the digs where the band was lodged near the Adelphi. The 'certainty of hazard' hadn't finished with me, however. Just a few yards down Lark Lane was an elderly upholsterer at work outside his shop on the webbing of an easy chair. ''Ullo, George dere,' he said, 'I used to do werk for yer mother.'

I saw Carole only twice more. I met her by appointment in the Bluecoat Chambers, a beautiful classical building, the front a courtyard and on the right-hand side a club called the Sandon, of which my parents were enthusiastic members. It was connected with the arts and at the back of the main block were studios. It was badly bombed in the war but luckily the damage was confined to the interior, leaving the beautiful façade unscathed. Faithfully and immediately reconstructed after the armistice, it now housed a coffee-bar, and it was there Carole and I met about midday – and her mother came too, a very nice lady.

Then, many years later, when we were doing a concert in the pub in the reconstituted Albert Dock (the Tate in the North, the Maritime Museum, expensive apartments and rather better than usual souvenir shops) the organizers told me there was someone to see me, and it was Carole, a decade or so on but looking wonderful. She seemed touched that I remembered her, but how could I have forgotten her?

11. 'Alas I Waver to and fro'

A woman is only a woman
But a good cigar is a smoke.
Rudyard Kipling

The quotation is, I'm sure, anathema to political correctness, and, resistant as I am to that finger-wagging, holier-than-thou bullying, even when I agree with its aim I still resent its obligatory surveillance. Any road, it is not my object here to dive into those troubled waters, but to describe my almost lifelong love affair with tobacco, even though at times I have tried, none too successfully, to dump it.

I have, of course, tried cigars, preferably little ones in tins or cardboard boxes, and I have fairly often accepted a large one. But I found the Whiffs and Hamlets not up to much, and the Corona Coronas and their Cuban competitors, very agreeable for the first puff or two, then became sodden in my mouth to the point of disintegration. So, despite the fact that Churchill and many tycoons favour them, it was back to gaspers for me.

For a time it was believed that, like pipes, roll-ups were less harmful than 'tailor-made' cigarettes, but lately these comforting myths have lost any credence. *All* tobacco is now officially bad for you. I'm sure it's true, so what am I doing lighting up? There are, I've noticed in passing, two principal classes who still smoke: teenagers, for whom it's a defiant gesture, and the old, who have always done it. As to class in general, smoking is less rejected at any age among the working classes, whereas the middle classes try and usually succeed in giving up.

As I'm not a teenager and, at seventy-eight, now puff away without guilt or inhibition, I must of course try to justify myself. I think a lot of it has to do with my adolescence and youth. It may be difficult to imagine it now, but in the twenties and thirties, or in my case the forties and fifties, to smoke was to appear glamorous and sophisticated. My maternal grandmother was mildly addicted to Gold Flakes, and her sons also. My father preferred Black Cats or Craven A, the latter of which was actually advertised as 'Good for the throat'. I don't think anybody, including doctors, believed that smoking was in any way life-threatening.

There were naturally class factors concerning what brand you smoked: full-length expensive ones for the bourgeoisie, short, cheap ones for the workers. The former usually filled their gold cigarette cases before leaving the house to dine out in the evening; the working classes usually favoured Wild Woodbines from the packet (and a very attractive packet it was, like a green and gold, art nouveau-ish, Turkish tile).

Most middle- and upper-middle-class households had large silver boxes, sometimes engraved with the names of their golf club and lined with a veneer of some scented wood, kept full of cigarettes for the convenience of guests. There were ashtrays, mostly of cut glass, on every table, including in the bedrooms.

Advertising of cigarettes was in all the newspapers and on many billboards. There was one brand named after Du

Maurier, the then famous actor whom my mother admired for his 'throw-away' effects. 'He could turn his back to the audience,' she'd tell me, admiringly, 'and you could tell what he was thinking.' The brand Du Maurier recruited famous figures of stage or screen with such slogans as, 'If Ivor Novello offered you a cigarette, it'd be a Du Maurier.'

Somebody expressed surprise that they hadn't chosen Godfrey Winn, the hideously sentimental and highly paid columnist. Noël Coward, who loathed 'Winifred God', as Winn was frequently nicknamed, mostly for his legendary meanness, intervened. 'If they did that,' he said, 'they'd have to change the wording to, "If Godfrey Winn offered you a cigarette [pause, no doubt perfectly judged] it'd be a fucking miracle!"'

Noël really did hate and despise 'Winifred'. When he died on the tennis court after one set too many to impress a brace of pretty boys who were his house guests, they, very emotionally, found his address book and eventually (I imagine with considerable difficulty) a full bottle of gin. Swigging this down after a weekend of near-abstention, they thought it appropriate to call up almost everybody listed, and eventually reached Coward's number in Switzerland, where he had long retired for tax reasons, and was also growing old and slightly feeble.

To protect his sleep he had no telephone in his bedroom. Woken in the small hours, he eventually heard it ringing in the hall, and for so long he felt it might be important. So, wearily, he got out of bed, put on one of the famous dressing-gowns, inserted and lit a cigarette in his holder, and shuffled downstairs. 'Yes?' he said (I should imagine his delivery even more clipped than usual).

'Oh, Sir Noël,' explained one of the two drunk youths emotionally, 'we thought we ought to let you know that poor Godfrey Winn is dead.'

'Good!' snapped Coward, banged the phone down and went back upstairs to catch up on his broken sleep.

The main incentive to start to smoke in my youth was the cinema. Watching old films on TV today, it's quite a shock to see how everyone puffs away: crooks, heroes, country gents, policemen and of course, once the war started, the armed forces. They were all at it all of the time, like experimental beagles in a laboratory. In battle, if someone was dying or badly wounded, the first thing his comrades did was to light one up and place it between his lips. 'Thanks, mate,' he'd usually say, if he could still speak.

I was born eight years after the end of the First World War. My mother's brothers, who had survived the conflict, were full of tales of the war and told me that cigarettes were as welcome as food parcels from those in Blighty, keeping the 'Home Fires Burning'. There were also references to smoking in some of the songs popular in the trenches and elsewhere. 'Pack Up Your Troubles in Your Old Kit Bag', for one, includes the following line: 'Whilst you've a Lucifer [a match] to light your fag, smile boys . . .'

In the twenties everyone, but bright young people especially, smoked away. In fact a cigarette, often in a holder, was as much part of their image as short skirts, make-up, bobbed hair and the Charleston. Much later, Humphrey Bogart was my example. He made it sexy and when he lit one and placed it between his heroine's lips, it was (during my testosterone years) totally seductive.

In the cinemas thereafter, far into the fifties and beyond, the air was grey with smoke, clearly to be seen in the beam of light carrying the image to the screen from the projection box high above the circle.

Then scientific research firmly tied the habit to terminal diseases. In America it has become banned almost everywhere. In France and Ireland, amazing in both cases, it is forbidden in all bars. Here, the prohibitions have been more gradual, but escalating all the time; and it's the sly manipulation, as slowly as a predator stalks a herbivore, that I especially resent. Examples: on buses, where you used to be able to smoke in the back seats upstairs, they have banned it totally. In the case of planes, too, to begin with the total ban was confined to short trips – now, to anywhere in the globe, whatever the distance. In most stations it's still allowed, except when they are below ground level, for example at Liverpool Street. Of course, the disastrous fire at King's Cross underground station made it easier to tighten the screws.

The majority of taxis are non-smoking and one very grumpy driver without a 'thank you for not smoking' sign told me it was up to him personally whether he allowed it or not, and he didn't. Many restaurants ban smokers. Most pubs don't bar it as yet, but the government has pledged to deny them that right if food is available. Airports have very small smoking areas – but for how long? Many office blocks, especially public buildings such as the BBC, have banned it and display notices telling you that 'This is a non-smoking building'. How, I wonder, does a building smoke?

Now don't imagine I haven't every sympathy with non- or anti-smokers; but surely, in fairness to the addicted, some smoking areas should be available. There is no sight so pathetic as those groups of people puffing frantically away outside buildings in the freezing cold or pouring rain. It is in those rare and decreasing areas where it is still permitted that I join what I have come to think of as 'the leper colony'.

There is no doubt that smoking is a threat to health, but surely those who decide to continue to do so should be allowed that choice. Some doctors refuse to treat heavy smokers. They claim, probably with some justification, that they fill up beds that should be available to non-smokers with serious or terminal complaints, but what of the gaga, the mindless, the 'old fools', an increasing number of whom also take up beds, doubly incontinent in many cases, unable to recognize anybody, their memories shot through? And what of alcoholics, their livers like inflated footballs? They too are surely an equal threat and often more aggressive than most smokers? What of petrol fumes which are just as lethal as nicotine, and are probably responsible for the hole in the ozone layer above the Arctic Circle?

This is not a defence of smoking. It's bad for you and should be limited, but the government, despite the enormous amount of money it gains from every packet, might act less slyly. I wonder, too, how many MPs smoke in secret? Are you old enough to remember when a pipe was considered a sign of being trustworthy? There was Baldwin, for a start, then Attlee and especially Harold Wilson (who, they say, in fact preferred cigars)?

Here finisheth my modified rant! Now I'm going to light a fag and drink a small Irish whiskey.

And, of course, in pulling out my packet of Marlboro Lites (I do know that the rugged young cowboy who used to advertise this brand died of lung cancer), I see that the gold and white packet has, on both sides and framed in black, an obligatory warning, 'Smoking seriously harms you and others around you' and on the other 'Stopping smoking reduces the risk of fatal heart and lung diseases'. I'm sure that's all true, but it lacks the more basic message on some packets 'Smoking kills', and that's certainly true too, but sometimes, especially after a few drinks, I take out my fibre-point pen and add, 'So does life'. Well, I don't smoke in non-smokers' cars, or around children, those with weak lungs, or even those who hate the smell of it, but I do smoke and I'll tell you how and why this happened, and why, too, I'm not trembling at my obstinate stupidity.

When I was at school in the early forties, and as camp as a row of tents, I used to smoke only Black Russian Sobranies (rolled in black paper with gold tips). Later, when I became interested in surrealism in general and Magritte in particular, I occasionally switched to Passing Clouds. The packet had a pink frame surrounding a table of cavaliers puffing away at surely anachronistic ciggies and the large but contained cloud above them bore the name Passing Cloud in letters formed from the smoke itself. We smoked Black Russians defiantly in our taxi on the day we left the school for the last time.

Actually J. F. Roxburgh, our dandified but remarkable headmaster, had drawled at us in an early briefing. Although he would be obliged to beat us if we were foolish enough to get caught, if we chose to smoke under one of the 2,408 shrubs in the grounds that was our affair. Indeed, so lightly was smoking taken at Stowe that many masters smoked in class, admittedly the majority favouring their 'trustworthy' pipes.

Still, for me smoking was a prop, not a real need.

It was the Navy which got me hooked. Duty-free tobacco was generously distributed, both in training camps and on sea-going ships, one of which, HMS *Dido*, a cruiser, I joined in Chatham, shortly after the war ended. We did little except goodwill cruises and rather uncomfortable exercises in the Bay of Biscay, mostly in very rough weather.

Here, certainly, the tobacco bonanza began. At regular intervals you were entitled to a large quantity of rolling baccy in an airproof tin (naturally they sold Rizla papers in the canteen and more luxuriously 'tailor mades' at seven old pence a packet). I became quite adept at making roll-ups and also owned a little machine to make it even easier and certainly neater. I, however, preferred tailor-made Gold Flakes when I was in sufficient funds.

There were strict, indeed draconian, rules about how much you were allowed to take ashore, depending on how long a leave you had. This was to stop you smuggling out enough to sell, at a huge profit in those years of fag shortage. Well I, and indeed most of the crew, didn't want to risk a spell in 'the glass house', a punishment barracks rumoured to be terrifyingly sadistic. On board, however, we were all chimneys in bell bottoms, although personally I never smoked when sailing because, while never sea-sick as such, I was always queasy.

I recall once, on the train to Liverpool, a rating sitting opposite me at one of the tables opened a whole pack of tailor-mades (presumably he was on long leave) and announced with great glee, 'I'm going ter smoke meself ter fookin' death!'

So I left 'the Andrew' (slang for the Royal Navy) hooked for life.

Moving to London to work for an art gallery at a tiny salary, I continued to puff away, but was often too broke to buy cigarettes even at the modest price then asked. I partially overcame this by collecting visitors' dog-ends, removing the cork tips and paper, and transferring the tobacco to a tin marked 'Poet's Mixture'. This delighted my boss, E. L. T. Mesens, although he claimed I wasn't thorough enough.

Then, when the gallery was closed down, I joined the jazz world, and spent about ten years with Mick Mulligan and we all smoked, even on stage. Like Mick I really did smoke. In fact, over the years I built up to seventy a day.

Diana also smoked heavily, but when her granddaughter Kezzie was born, she decided to give up. She undertook hypnosis treatment and, after a considerable struggle, succeeded. She had rolled her own for as long as I could remember, and sometimes asked me to roll one for her in the car on our way to Wales. Her reasons for stopping were completely understandable. She sometimes got bronchitis and both her father and mother had died of lung cancer within a very short time of each other.

Ten years ago I was ordered by the doctors in Colchester General Hospital to give up when I nearly died of a bleeding ulcer. Diana bought me a doodling pad, coloured pens and sweets, but when my ulcer was cured with a powerful cocktail of antibiotics I started again. Then six years ago I had bronchial pneumonia. I went in to St Mary's, was diagnosed with COPD (chronic obstructive pulmonary disease) and was given oxygen at frequent intervals. I didn't understand why so many close friends came to visit me, but later came to the conclusion it was because Diana thought I was going to die.

But then I didn't.

Once the novelist Penelope Mortimer came to lunch. She smoked non-stop, although she'd already had one lung removed, with the excuse that it had taken sixty years to account for that and so it would take about the same again before the other one went – a curiously unrealistic belief, and indeed she died very soon afterwards.

I'm very fond of delicious food, but would eat my dinner rather quickly and then wait – how gallantly – until Diana, a much slower chewer and swallower, had finished. But I would already have a cigarette in one hand and my lighter in the other, and she found it extremely irritating – and let me know it.

Once I'd had my bronchitis attack, she insisted I went to be hypnotized, as it had helped her; and I agreed.

There is a man called Allen Carr who is famous for curing tobacco addiction. I didn't see him but his assistant, who practised in a distant suburb. Having learnt the business at his master's knee, he struck me as very logical and efficient, as well as practising a clever psychological trick. He was also, of course, a hypnotist of music-hall proficiency.

Diana was told when she made the appointment that I should bring with me a packet of my preferred brand of cigarettes. When I got there and was facing my very nice interrogator and lecturer, I saw that in his consulting room there was a couch, but, most remarkably, facing his desk in the corner was a huge pyramid of cigarette packets containing enough fags, I worked out later, to last a chain-smoker a lifetime of puffing away. By my side was a large ashtray.

The psychological trick was that I was told to smoke as much as I wanted to, while he began to talk, calmly and rationally, about why I should give up. I had to agree with every word he said.

Smoking was not a pleasure; smokers thought it was, but in fact, as with any other drug, it was an addiction. Smokers simply ignored this, but of course they persisted in deceiving themselves that only satisfaction was involved and they needed the reassuring ritual of lighting up.

Excuses for this need were diverse: anxiety, happiness, boredom, pleasure, good news, bad news, just wanting one, social ease, companionship, after eating, on the loo, after making love. I'm not sure that I didn't imagine the last, but it was certainly one of *my* excuses. I thought of a post-coital cigarette as 'a parachute between erotic ecstasy and ordinary reality'. I am sure, too, now it's no longer a problem, that I didn't think I could handle an affair with anyone who didn't smoke, easier said and done in those less lung-conscious days.

He spoke of the duplicity of the cigarette manufacturers, who, now that anti- and non-smoking opinion must have meant a considerable reduction in their profits, unload massive amounts of fags into the Third World, and their determination to find loopholes in the escalating ban on tobacco advertising and sponsorship.

This is what I can remember of the gist of what he said, but it may well include items of my own invention. He was entirely convincing, and throughout I smoked like a man with his last cigarette before ascending the scaffold. When he'd finished talking he asked me to smoke one last 'coffin nail' before he hypnotized me. Then he told me to throw what remained of the packet on to the pyramid in the corner. Not that many left, I noticed when about to launch the parabola into my fag-packet cemetery. Not many at all! Came the hypnosis, I went out like a light and woke feeling new-born and tobacco-free.

For several days I suffered no temptation, but then, seeing someone I knew in my local getting a cigarette out, I asked him if he could spare one and he said 'Of course' and it tasted marvellous. I was again hooked and used this poncing technique for some time. Only once was I refused. A gruff Northerner in the bar attached to the golf club near the lake where I used to fish said 'No – buy your own' and quite soon after that I began to, but only ten at a time, when I was out of the cottage. Then I took to leaving a packet behind the counter in the local pub and asking for one, but only when I needed it.

At that time I tried to hide my lapsing from my wife with the use of a product called Gold Spot, a small spray that concealed all 'odours on the breath'. It seemed, however, that she'd begun to be suspicious. What, she asked me, was the pile of matches in my bathroom doing stacked behind my tooth-mug? I told her my mother had claimed they destroyed 'unpleasant odours after an Eartha Kitt'. Even so, Diana had noticed how often in London I was visiting the local at odd times of the day.

The denouement came when I was invited to speak at a conference on art and business in Belfast. I spoke entirely on art, having as much aptitude and indeed enthusiasm for business as a solitary anchovy. By this time, when not in London or Berkshire, I'd given up even trying, and during one of the most boring and suspect lectures on buying art for profit, I sneaked out through a side entrance and sat on a concrete block near the water smoking a much-craved Sweet Afton (I always support the *tabac du pays*, Gauloises in France, for example).

What I didn't know was that, under a wet leather hat like a cow-pat and, very bent to ease my back, under a heavy coat of the same origin, I was giving a good impression of Quasimodo. I was unaware that a press photographer, recognizing a grotesque image, had taken several pictures, one of which appeared on the front page of an Ulster paper days after I'd gone with my name printed underneath it.

Among the other participants at the conference was an old friend, the novelist, fashion editor and columnist Polly Devlin, married now for many years to my old flatmate of the fifties, Andy Garnett. On my last evening we had had a jolly booze-up in a huge hotel, as security-minded as an Iraqi police station, and directly opposite a beautiful Victorian pub (unspoilt) where some of the action of that great film *Odd Man Out* took place. I smoked, but told Polly that I tried to keep it secret from Diana.

After I'd gone back to London the 'Patience Sitting on a Monument Smoking' photograph appeared, and Polly sent it to me with a joke about being able to blackmail me if she threatened to tell Diana. What she didn't know was that Diana, being in charge of the business side of my life and supervisor of my professional engagements as well (the latter often confused by me, especially as my latest 'senior moment' is to forget what date it is), opens all my post if it hasn't got 'Personal' written on the envelope.

Shock! Horror! And confrontation! It was irrefutable evidence, the equivalent of a knock-me-down clue in a TV detective or legal drama which, produced at the last moment in court, reveals the real villain.

For a start Diana was furious with Polly about the joke and it was a long time before they made it up. As for me, after a real dressing down (justified, I have to agree), she sent me back to the hypnotist for another brainwash.

It was like the second take of a scene in a movie, only this time my part in it was less convincing. I had doubts before going into the room, but felt obliged to give it a whirl.

Take Two: the man behind the desk, the couch (or was it an adjustable easy chair for the hypnotic sequence?), the pyramid, even higher than before, the almost identical lecture which, if I had taken his place I could have delivered myself, largely because I agreed with everything he said, the packet of Benson and Hedges, the brand I had taken to, the heavy, hopefully final near-chain-smoke, the disposal on command of the packet, the easy slide into a mesmerized state of unconsciousness.

This time I came to convinced, but less so than before, that it had (or might) have worked. My instructor was opening the window to clear at least a little of the smoke I was responsible for.

I said I certainly didn't want a cigarette and would try harder this time to avoid giving in. I thanked him and was about to leave the room to pay the bill (quite hefty, but it would soon have been covered by the money I'd save by not adding to the profits of Benson and Hedges) when he said something so perspicacious as to give me pause. 'Yes,' he said. 'Well I hope this time it really does take, only,' he told me, 'you're a rebel.'

Rebel? The word is perhaps, over romantic for me. Che Guevara I'm not. What I am, though, is obstinate, sometimes provoked into anger by stupidity, deceit, bullying and my own conviction. I supported, fairly actively on occasion, CND, homosexual rights, the legalization of soft drugs, anti-apartheid and the right to early abortion. As you see, a typical liberal list. I have, too, on occasion, acted out of personal rather than public reasons. I am also a convinced atheist. Of none of this I'm ashamed, but I lie quite often, partially to escape hurting people but also to avoid, usually at the same time, heavy confrontations or doing something I don't want to.

So, of course, not so long after my second session, I again started smoking, at first asking smokers to spare me one, then buying first ten, then twenty cigarettes, and was, I forget quite how, found out again.

Diana had been cured of arachnophobia by another healing guru, this time a young American, practising in Windsor, and I said I'd see him. So from Newbury I went to Windsor and there was the very agreeable Yank. As I left, he gave me a tape he'd recorded of our session. The end of it is this: 'George, you weren't born with a cigarette in your mouth and you won't die with one either.' Would that both parts were true! Even as I left him – and I'd liked him a lot – I recognized that my fall from a state of nicotine-free grace would not be long. I sat in a café in the shadow of Windsor Castle, drank a coffee, ate a Danish pastry and wished I was opening a new pack and holding a match or lighter to a cigarette. Diana had lost.

Back in London on TV, Nic O'Teen, a predictably demonic figure, strove with an addicted teenager. For more grown-up smokers, a pretty girl physically set about a five-foot ciggy with a silly face and eventually knocked it, bent double, into a dustbin. Then there was a cheerful person wearing yellow rubber gloves washing up. The commentator told us that after eating is the most likely time to give in and advised us to do something to take our minds off it. Washing up, for instance: impossible to smoke while wearing wet rubber gloves. Finally there were two young lovers about to kiss, I got the impression in a cinema, but surely there I am mistaken, as it is prohibited. At all events, on contact she immediately pulls back and tells him in disgust, and with a predictable Estuary accent: 'You tyest like aneshtry.' I don't think that even smokers, certainly not me, would lick out an ashtray for pleasure.

I am remembering these attempts to lead us into a smoke-less universe and to help recover our sense of taste and smell. There is, however, a fake solution available at any chemist, a small if rather expensive tube called Gold Plus. It used to be red or green (mint) but now, in my recent experience, it's black. Whatever the colour, it has a gold cap to justify its trade-name, which makes it look really expensive, as though it were a phial of a scent so pricey as to be saleable to all but millionairesses only in such a Lilliputian container.

To reinforce this illusion, when you remove the top there is a black push-button spray with a small white hole on one side. This you direct towards your open mouth and press down the knob at the top. I give it three squirts and it does exactly what it promises. It also kills the reek of garlic, curry and certainly the ashtray effect. I've known people to recognize it or ask what it is that's making my breath smell so medicinal (it is quite assertive), but I have never known anyone say 'You've been smoking', and even the girl rejecting the attentions of the young man might have been deceived.

About bad breath as such I can't say much because so few people are prepared to tell you, or you them. There are, however, exceptions even here. For instance, in the fifties an Australian jazz band arrived here fronted by Graeme Bell on trumpet. It was an enormous success on its first visit, less so on its second appearance when the revivalist boom was beginning to fade somewhat.

They brought with them on both occasions a manager called Mel Langdon, a man who knew no fear. In Sheffield, when he was interviewed by a local journalist, a very tall, perfectly agreeable man, but famous throughout the British jazz world for his constant five-star bad breath, Mel found himself trapped in a corner of the dressing-room. This unfortunate 'journo' (Oz slang) furthermore had an unfortunate habit, being so tall, of leaning forward.

Now British jazz musicians, while quite prepared to joke viciously about this man's physical handicap, would never have dreamed of bringing it to his attention. Mel Langdon had no such inhibitions. 'I say, old man,' he observed, 'your Macbeth's a bit tragic!' This observation was overheard by several British 'musos' (another Oz abbreviation) and took no time to spread, like an Australian bush fire, throughout our ranks. Relieved at last by Mel's frankness, we felt like medieval princesses rescued by a courageous (rather rude) knight facing a fire-breathing dragon.

Shortened to 'tragic Macbeth', it gave us at least a comical expression for this widespread complaint, although British kindness or cowardice (take your choice) still inhibits us from instantly informing the unconscious offender of his rotting gums or faulty digestive tract. What we fear is umbrage and resentment, just as most of us feel if accused of having too much hair sprouting from our ears or nostrils.

In a longish and what my paternal grandmother called a dissipated life, I have only been told once that my Macbeth was tragic and that was eight years before I smoked consistently, so it must have been intestinal. In a classroom at Stowe, sitting next to an exceptionally beautiful boy, I said something, presumably flirtatious, and he, with the voice of a drill sergeant ordering a new conscript to get his hair cut, told me to face the other way if I wanted to say anything to him.

I was surprised, shocked and ashamed, but it had an effect. I brushed my teeth, gargled and, even if I didn't need to, I would each morning heave and strain in what Stoics call (or called, in my time) 'Egypt'. It gained this rather odd appellation because, under the steps leading up to the grand entrance of the North Front, a rather whimsical early nineteenth-century architect had designed a foyer in the Egyptian manner: hieroglyphics, columns à la Hoover factory and a lavatory. Naturally enough it was this that earned the loo its appropriate nickname, which soon spread throughout the school and was not uniquely applied to its original source. As a result the very name Egypt, used outside its lavatorial context, reduced most Stoics to ill-controlled giggles.

Both the Old and New Testaments were dangerous territories. To take just two examples, in the Old Testament, Moses led the Jews *out* of Egypt, in the New the Holy Family fled *into* it. Max Miller would have been proud of the hysterical, if suppressed, laughter these harmless tales provoked.

Even today, over sixty years later, the mention of Egypt on a news bulletin can raise a smile. I wonder if all Old Stoics find it to have the same effect?

Once more the WingCo caught me out. This was when I was going to bed, probably after a nightcap, or eight. I left half a packet of Marlboro Lites lying in neat alignment with a lighter with lips on it, on the writing table in my bedroom. (I wasn't, however, 'elevated', as the Regency port-swiggers termed it.)

I didn't even try to defend myself this time, and only a day or two later we set out together to see Dr Kohn, my lung man.

First I had to have another scan. Yet again I was ordered to hold my breath, breathe out as fast as I could and then do it all again, but normally. Throughout, as before, like a *son et lumière* show, a psychedelic necklace flicked along the narrow gutter towards the top of the tube from which either one's head or feet projected, like a girl in a conjurer's act about to be sawn in two.

Dr Kohn first examined the new X-rays and compared them with those on my last visit. My second white spot on the lungs had, unlike the first, not disappeared between appointments. It was therefore still suspect, but without inserting a syringe big enough to knock out an adult African bull elephant in musk, there was no way to be certain. As before, I refused any physical intervention, but wanted to know if it had increased in size. 'Yes,' said Dr Kohn looking at both X-rays side by side, 'but at most a millimetre.'

Although unable to memorize any Euro-revision of weights and measures, I gathered at least that this was a minimal growth.

As for my other threatener, emphysema, it too, while still there slopping about in the bottom of my lungs, was under control, my breathing (thanks, I'm sure, to my multi-coloured puffers) steady and free from wheezing.

I told him, confirmed by the WingCo as if reporting an airman's serious offence to a superior officer, that I was smoking again.

Dr Kohn didn't explode as certain doctors would have done. It was my decision, he told me. Better if I didn't, but he knew I refused to take several months off for an operation; and it was doubtful anyway if a surgeon would consent to perform one with my irregular heartbeat and other conceivably damaging factors. He took in also that at seventy-eight I was determined to enjoy myself rather than tremble and shake before the future. Diana, perhaps with reluctance (but at least she had tried her best to wean me off lighting up), accepted what he'd said.

He also added, rather reassuringly, that if I became really ill my present intransigence would in no way affect any future treatment.

We then had a little chat about the recent jazz night in a rather Hammer-film-Gothic nightclub for the benefit, appropriately enough, of St Mary's cancer research. Dr Kohn wanted to know whether I would appear at their next one, almost a year ahead. 'Of course,' I said, and for nothing as before. After all, I owe a great deal to that hospital and besides, Dr Kohn's belief that I'd be here to attend cheered me up no end.

So from then on I have smoked openly but, given that Diana hates the smell of it, in the house I do so only in my bedroom at the top, leave a window wide open, and confine myself, although not exclusively, to my own little Egypt behind a tight-sliding door.

I have added several anti-stale ashtray devices and various precautions. The first is to smoke sitting on the loo with the lid down and blow the smoke into the steam from the turned on hot tap in the adjacent basin. This rises towards a small air-extractor above the cistern, carrying, I hope, the cigarette smoke with it. Then, switching off the hot tap, I turn on the cold one to extinguish my dog-end, prior to throwing it far into the road. This is a skill I have gradually perfected, and quite often I succeed in actually landing it in the gutter. (When I achieve this not too difficult feat, I congratulate myself in an accent suggestive of windmills, tulips, clogs, soft drugs and legalized prostitution. *'In der gute'* is a straight translation into Dutch. I know this because in the seventies, when we were appearing in Amsterdam, on the edge of the pavements was the representation of a dog in silhouette engaged in heaving and straining and beneath it this brusque command to move its arse five inches to the right or left.)

My other precaution is to expel several squirts from an air-freshener, a device which certainly masks the smell of tobacco smoke but in no way eliminates it. The names of these products are equally ridiculous: they promise the illusion of an Alpine glen, or a hillside of lily of the valley, whereas they smell of synthetic chemicals; in fact they smell like what my father used to call 'a whore's boudoir' (how did *he* know?).

When I explained to Diana my apparently thoughtful attempts to freshen the air, she objected. It involved, she said, a waste of hot water and, worse, the release of a disgusting smell which didn't obliterate smoke but only masked it. OK, I agreed, but I still employ both water and spray for my own gratification, and if I time it right, when she comes back from the cottage, the traces of both the Alpine glade and the money-wasting hot water have evaporated, leaving the doubtful air of Shepherd's Bush in its place.

Recently on TV I saw an advert for a new air-freshener which first dismisses its rivals for, as Diana had already asserted, only masking 'offensive odours', then claims it *destroys* them. I'm going to try this out as soon as I can find it. As yet – I hope it is not due to pressure from its rivals – it seems unknown to the many chemists I've asked about it.

One sunny afternoon in a Birmingham garden attached to the house of Professor and Mrs Hoggart, he spoke of an aunt who hated the smell of human excrement. Then she discovered the scented sprays and for a time believed she had found a permanent solution, but then she started to associate the sweet smell of the sprays with the human stink they hid and so in the end was no better off.

A final statement on my current position on smoking: my only rule is that, if I run out of cigarettes at home, I never walk to the newsagent at the end of the road especially to stock up, but wait until I have to go out for medicinal or professional reasons; and then, with all the excitement of a prisoner breaking parole, I walk to the nearest pub, buy a Stella Artois if available and a whiskey and ritualistically, like a priest at the altar, slowly open the packet, extract the first neat cylinder and light up. That very first puff is the best. I

'I am and will remain a true and happy smoker'

sit there in a kind of pleasurable trance, ignoring the cackling and triumphant capering of Nic O'Teen and his allies. I am and will remain a true and happy smoker. Oscar Wilde put it best (when didn't he?): 'Smoking is the only perfect vice – because it's never satisfied.'

12. Treats

About suffering they were never wrong
The Old Masters, how well they understood
Its human position . . .

W. H. Auden

I must stop banging on about my health (although no doubt
I shall issue a short communiqué after my next appointment
with Dr Kohn), and instead write positively of those pleasures which remain and which I think of now as 'treats',
that is to say, those invitations or events I cannot, nor would
want to, resist. I usually pay the price of feeling absolutely
destroyed afterwards. The only solution then is to 'climb the
wooden stairs to Bedfordshire', as old-fashioned nannies
used to say (and may still do), or 'hit the sack', or 'wanking
chariot', as Mick Mulligan preferred to describe it.

My most recent 'treat' was the Caravaggio exhibition at
the Sainsbury Wing of the National Gallery. The exterior of
this extension is a bland affair, but the original design didn't
please the Prince of Wales. He described it as 'like a car-
buncle on the face of a dear friend', and I'm sure most of
the public with their mistrust of extreme modern architec-
ture would be on his side. I really despise what they finally
put up. It nicked several features of the 'dear friend' next
door – classical columns, architectural details and the like –
and then gradually simplified and eventually erased them

altogether, as if with an India rubber. On the other hand I find the interior, while austere, perfectly OK. All its galleries, including the one in the basement, are tall, the lighting versatile, and there is enough hanging space. The late Caravaggios certainly need that space, the majority of them being enormous.

I had tried to visit this show earlier, but seeing the long queues outside I had calculated that, even if I'd waited, the sardine-like crowd would make it impossible to get back far enough to see a whole picture or near enough to grasp the significant naturalistic detail: the dirty feet, the broken nails, the frayed sleeves. And the faces too: the 'job's-worth' torturers, Salomé's expression, arising from sexual frustration and its subsequent kinky satisfaction, holding up the head of John the Baptist, whom she had failed to seduce but whose dead mouth she was now at liberty to kiss.

Out of the dark of all this shabby splendour emerge images to solidify in shafts of light. A hand, thrust out towards us, creates the illusion of a third dimension. Yet perhaps the most amazing work in the whole exhibition is the almost sensual slump of Christ, a bead of blood beginning to trickle down his forehead from the recently jammed on crown of thorns.

When I arrived in London just after the war I made a point of visiting all the interesting exhibitions at the museums and private galleries but there were only a few (even the Picasso and Matisse shows) where you couldn't slide in easily enough. Today, I sometimes wonder how much the 'been there, done that' mob really likes pictures. Certainly art is no longer confined to a few artists, their educated and intellectual admirers and sincere collectors. Art is now 'cool'. If it's real enthusiasm, that's fine. If it's a passing fad, like the yo-yo or art deco, well it will pass. I don't mind either way.

I believe that if you love and understand art as such you've been lucky. But if, for example, you worship 'the beautiful game', then that's fine by me too, and the same applies to a penchant for motors or even cricket. All I ask is that the fans of these various enthusiasms don't take it for granted that everybody shares their obsessions, and I, in my turn, will try to avoid bending their ears on surrealism, jazz and fishing.

I do, however, deplore that television companies seem concerned only with maximum viewing figures, and have been dumbing down their programmes in general and those of minority interests in particular. There is very little covering the arts, although I understand that Channel 5 is preparing to cut back on the 'tits 'n' arse'. I have to admit that I occasionally like a bit of 'tits 'n' arse', and at the time when I was too ill to read or concentrate I could enjoy any kind of rubbish; and still do if overtired, a bit pissed or both. I don't think it's an either/or situation; I don't believe that everybody is either only high-brow or low-brow. But where are the great informative series? Where, for example, is the admirable Robert Hughes, the Oz narrator and writer of *The Shock of the New*? Witty he was, and no doubt is still. He was a wild boy in the sixties and a grizzled sage today. He's also infinitely funnier and no less irreverent than most contemporary 'alternative' comics with their obsession with wanking. Where (wait for it) are the Morecambe and Wise of today? A typical old codger remark that, but then I am one, after all. Pomposity and 'the grass is greenerism' are the hallmarks of most old men's pronouncements. Alienating and boring both, no doubt.

What I really like is nature red in tooth, claw and fanny, although I don't think any commentator has come along to challenge the informative David Attenborough as master of cool even when in the arms of a silver-backed male gorilla.

There are, it's true, several rangy girls touchingly obsessed with the slim survival chances of cheetah cubs, and some rather serious neutral men of the same mind, but there is also a young Australian who, while obviously courageous and offering confidence and expertise, drives me mad with irritation. He has blond hair and very macho shorts which show off more leg than a pole dancer. He also describes the most dangerous creatures as if they were 'beaut Sheilas'. 'What a little beauty,' he says, manhandling a particularly venomous viper doing its best to inject his bare arm, and he loves physical involvement and risk with huge and bad-tempered 'crocs'. He's more like a showman than a guide, although I will admit he's calmed down a bit recently – and not before time.

Otherwise, apart from snooker and women playing tennis, my only 'can't miss' programme is *The Antiques Road Show*, the Chippendale daddy of them all. It's not entirely enjoyable, but while one learns from experts whether the legs are 'right', or how to tell an Edwardian copy from the real thing, it is the varied reaction of the people who've turned up with a treasure which is really fascinating. Here the upper-middle-class woman's response to being told that her great-grandmother's escritoire is worth thousands is as unexcited as if a not especially good cook had given her notice. This is in direct contrast with the near hysteria of a working-class woman whom the experts tell that the Chinese vase her great-uncle brought back from Hong Kong during his service in the Merchant Navy, and which has recently been stored in the cupboard under the stairs, is of eighteenth-century origin and worth several thousands. 'No! You're having me on!' screams the plumber's wife incredulously. She then laughs hysterically and, partially covering her mouth, repeats the sum several times. She doesn't bother to listen to what it should be insured for, and one senses that as soon as possible, having given it long enough time to swank to the neighbours, it'll be on its way to the auction room – and why not?

But then, perhaps the upper-middle-class couple in their well-worn tweeds may decide to do exactly the same thing in order to repair the roof on their Grade II Georgian home.

My favourite and deeply unpleasant joke on the subject came from Bernard Manning, an outstanding comedian when it comes to timing his inevitably dodgy material. Asked what would give him the maximum pleasure, he said it would be to appear as an expert on the *Road Show* and (his voice softened) a dear old lady, obviously badly off, would open a cardboard box and unwrap a small framed mirror. Manning would examine it in detail and then ask her if she wanted to know what it was worth. 'Oh yes,' she would cry, trying to conceal her excitement. 'Well,' Piggy would say, 'it's worth FUCK ALL!'

Another senior moment, I'm afraid. I look back a few pages to see where I left the straight road. Caravaggio! Could it have been?

*

So, to return finally to my evening with the slumping Christ, how did I, put off by the vast crowds, get to see it? I know I would, in the end, have 'stood the buffet with knaves that smelt of sweat'. Although in fact the crowds today aren't knaves, nor would they have smelt of sweat. It is only very occasionally, unlike in my youth, that you come across people who are strangers to deodorants, except for trampish alcoholics. I read, however, that Elizabethans were often excited by sweat, despite Shakespeare's adverse opinion. Mulligan wasn't against it either, in an erotic context. He called it 'a healthy pong'. I think too that it was appreciated by the beruffled gallants and their female contemporaries for the same aphrodisiac reasons. It would seem that Lord Darnley was implored by his friends never to change his shirt on account of his BO's powerful appeal.

There was no need, however, for me to brave the physical and mental strain of the crush. I'd heard that, after closing to the general public, the gallery would open for two hours to allow artists a clear view of the pictures. The lovable, eccentric and remarkable painter Craigie Aitchison, ARA, sent me and a 'long-time friend' a letter of invitation and we sailed in.

My 'long-time friend', despite occasional rows and 'non-speakers', had known him for so many years that she always referred to him as 'the fiancé'. Her nickname is Greckel, not her real nickname, but I asked Diana to change it in her book (already published by the time you'll read this), as she is her relentless enemy, and so I will use that name now. Craigie didn't come with us that evening. He had been to an earlier 'special evening' and found it almost as full as usual.

That night there was no danger of that. Most of the artists were middle-aged but well known. Many of them I knew. I was especially pleased to meet again Frank Auerbach whom I had not seen for many years, and who was as friendly as if we had last talked together the week before in the Colony Room.

My reaction to the work of that vicious and quarrelsome queen and genius, Caravaggio, I have already described. Afterwards Greckel and I had supper together, although it ended badly. After a bottle of saki (and we had both had a few drinks earlier) I became rather pompous and started criticizing her several destructive traits (pomposity is one of the major dangers of old age) and she, when she'd had enough of me and the saki, left the Chinese restaurant in a huff. Of course we rang each other up the next day and both apologized. We love each other too much not to.

I remain for ever grateful to Craigie for arranging our attendance at the exhibition via the director of the National Gallery. His passion for painting is the equivalent of the lifelong driven obsession of Matisse. His naiveté in day-to-day life pays off against most odds in his favour. When I first knew him I likened him to a fox, but no more. He is a driven man. His take on the world is as fanatical as any business tycoon's but it is much more sympathetic. Recently, in Tuscany where he owns an underfurnished former farm, Greckel told him that in the local market it was customary to bargain. Craigie took this in apparently, but on his next visit put it into practice by doubling the prices asked for aubergines, say, or a loaf of bread. This of course astounded and shocked the market traders. 'You want two!' they cried in disbelieving frustration. It was close to Derek Taylor's insistence on offering more and more for the Glaswegian's banal lighter, but for Derek it was out of conscious mischief, in Craigie's case from a genuine misunderstanding of what 'bargaining' implied.

Some years ago Craigie was awarded a CBE and went along to Buckingham Palace with Greckel to receive it. Craigie has a large head with long but beautifully presented white hair. He dresses colourfully. His face is as changeable and unreadable as a baby's. Will it cry? Will it laugh? His voice, with just a tinge of Scots accent, is high-pitched. His head nods quite often, he shuffles, as I do, rather than strides out. His house, inherited from his mother, has rather good furniture, brightly regilded, and its walls decorated in his favourite colours, shades of pink especially. Every flat surface is covered with kitsch, mostly broken ornaments transformed as if by a magician into glittering treasures. He loves dogs obsessively, especially Bedlingtons, of which he owns several. He often wears a T-shirt on which is printed 'Bedlingtons are best'.

Here, with some guilt, I find myself unable, as I so often am (another increasing and regrettable tendency of age), to resist inserting a joke of my father's. An Italian is criticizing his best friend: 'You come in da house, you eata alla da spaghetti, you drinka alla da chianti, you fucka da wife, you knocka da Jesus Christ offa da mantelpiece and breaka da legs. One day, ma friend, YOU GO TOO FAR!'

Greckel dresses in a very personal way too, not at all identical to the fiancé, but with a shared love of pink. The two of them must have looked quite odd at the palace, like slightly dishevelled tropical birds surrounded by formal rooks and magpies.

When it was Craigie's turn to approach the Queen, I imagine she must have glanced at her list to see what he actually did. After all, HM isn't noted, despite owning one of the best collections in the world, for being very interested in art and especially, unlike her late mother, contemporary art. If Craigie had been a jockey it would have been different. She has no obligation to prefer painting to racing, but I can't see her spending a spare evening leafing through her unique drawers full of Leonardo drawings at Windsor Castle. Still, she always fulfils her obligations.

When he shuffled forward she said, 'I see you're a painter, Mr Aitchison. What are your favourite subjects?'

This encounter he described immediately after receiving his medal to the naturally curious Greckel, who asked him how he'd answered the Queen's polite question.

'Jesus Christ, black people and doggies,' he'd told her. She hadn't commissioned him to paint the corgies, however.

There is nothing whimsical or affected in calling his Bedlingtons 'doggies'. He never calls them anything else. Nor is he religious, as far as I know, despite the fact that he paints JC so often and has been commissioned by several churches. Not being much of a draughtsman, he usually paints Christ without arms, although often comforted by little birds and sometimes with a Bedlington at the foot of the cross.

He once was given an exhibition in Monte Carlo, although naturally the French couldn't see his point. One day a critic approached him. 'Why do you h'always paint h'our Lerd wizout erms?' he asked him. Craigie answered with irritated dignity, 'Not everybody is born with arms, you know.' Greckel told me this.

Whether provoked by this impertinence or perhaps shaken by how often this question was put to him, the painter has quite often since given his Christs 'erms'. I feel it's not a significant improvement, as they are usually far too long and drape over the cross-beam rather than being nailed to it. But for me they are just as beautiful.

My next treat, just by chance, also involved Buck House. I got an invitation from the Queen and her saloon-bar philistine of a consort to 'an evening's celebration of British Music'. With my fear of being charmed, swallowed and digested by the Establishment, I asked my manager to find out if Lyttelton was going. 'I think you should make up your own mind,' said the WingCo; but I needed Humph's say-so. That is because he, by birth related to many grand families, has always turned down what I'm sure has been the offer of many honours, including, I dare say, a life peerage. He has refused them all, remaining faithful to his left-wing rejection of his heritage, although he still retains the perfect manners and accent of his origins. 'Yes,' he told my agent Jack Higgins, and so I, who was cat-like with curiosity anyway, felt it possible to accept.

My new house-sharer Mark agreed to drive me there, an official clearance sticker on his windscreen. Although I'd warned him I'd no way to get him in, he was still curious enough to park in the official car park in the central courtyard, taking with him one of his approved religious books. We sailed through. No doubt being black, in these PC days, probably ensured his easy passage. At the entrance I was greeted as 'George' by several policemen and officials in charge. A lot of the more mature ones do this, some of them because they're jazz lovers or because they've seen me on TV. This has often happened in recent years, even though, on *Room 101*, the royal family were one of my successful choices for the drop, (the others were swans and Boyz Bands). 'Bad for your street cred,' said my friend and one-time lover Louisa Buck, but it doesn't seem to have made any difference there.

Inside, up an impressive staircase with royal ancestors on both walls, I entered a series of huge rooms with enough gilt to satisfy Craigie on his earlier visit, and more dodgy monarchs two deep *in situ*. The canapés weren't up to much but there were ashtrays on every valuable flat surface. (I don't suppose even Blair will have the right to ban these – another reason among many for hoping he'll never be elected Life-President.) Even better, instead of the usual reception glasses of ferret's piss or red ink, there were bottles of good whiskey and pretty obliging boys to replenish my glass.

The musicians present were largely, I suspect, classical conductors, composers and soloists (I'm an ignoramus, a philistine, when it comes to 'serious music'), but I did meet and chat with a charming couple, not in the first flush of youth although much younger than I, who give singing recitals of whatever is required including Gilbert and Sulli-van, a love of which I have inherited from my father, he from his Victorian relatives.

Otherwise, I saw no jazz musicians except H. Lyttelton. Like 'Pussy cat, Pussy cat', we both saw the Queen and Phil the Greek in the distance. There were people all round them and passing in front of them, hoping for a smile or a word, but neither Humph nor I joined the oboists or conductors.

Humph told me that when he was a trainee Guards officer stationed in Windsor, he was sometimes detailed off with a colleague to dance with the two princesses at the Castle. As they, especially Margaret Rose, were quite short and he over six foot with enormous feet (size thirteen, I think), and as furthermore most jazz musicians are not usually adept at strictly ballroom, he told me he never enjoyed it.

When people started to leave I followed their example, and Mark drove me back to Shepherd's Bush for supper. I can't say I hadn't been fascinated, but then, though no royalist, I always read everything about the House of Windsor, just as, while no Catholic, I watched the last hours and subsequent funeral of the Pope. When he was editor of *Punch*, Alan Coren, on hearing that the Holy Pole had been named 'John Paul the Second', suggested the next one should be installed as 'George Ringo'. Well, my crimson cardinals, now, while black smoke still belches from the Vatican chimney, is your chance to follow this up! But I don't suppose you'll take it.

My Cinderella-like visit to the Palace is over, and I doubt it will be repeated. (How my mother would have milked it for all it was worth, using a special offhand voice she always adopted to swank about her children.) Now that I've shaken the gold-dust of the Palace carpets from my shoes, I should mention some other invitations which, without Humph, I always attend whenever I can: One: the Ian Macintosh Memorial Lunch and Good-time Afternoon. I'm aware that most people, apart from those who remember the fifties and sixties jazz world, won't know who Ian Macintosh was, nor why his passing should be remembered with an annual lunch. He was a timber merchant living in Cuffley, very conventional in most ways but also a Louis Armstrong fanatic and a rather loud good disciple of his hero, but unfortunately tending to blow increasingly louder and eventually all over the place when in his cups. I don't know how far in the past lay his Scottish roots, but apart from being called Macintosh, and the names he gave his sons, there was no trace of them. Indeed the same is true of most upper-middle- and upper-class Scots that I have known. One of his sons you may indeed have heard of. His name is Cameron, the millionaire producer of many worldwide musical hits of recent years, *Les Misérables* for example.

There is one story which neatly encapsulates the two sides of Ian and 'Spike', as he was nicknamed in his Satchmo persona. It was at a party at Wally Fawkes's large white house near Swiss Cottage during his younger and wilder days, when he was still with Sandy, his first and raving wife. We were all, including Ian, punishing the drink, and, as often then, a jam session materialized. Ian metamorphosed easily into Spike and began, as the booze worked its black magic, to blow at top volume and finished an LP-length solo with the usual disintegrating multiple coda.

He'd blown so loudly as to wake Wal and Sandy's two young daughters and they'd got up to see what was going on. They were leaning on the top banister. Spike spotted them and immediately returned to Ian. 'Wally,' he growled, 'shouldn't those children be in bed?'

You could be confident about Spike's reaction to any situation. Once, in the fifties, there was a convention of timber merchants in London and Spike was expected to arrange some entertainment. From somewhere he heard of a detective inspector who, assisted by a policeman with a projector and a constable in uniform to rewind the films in the kitchen, could provide 'a nice evening's entertainment', as Dame Edna puts it. The detective inspector said yes – I presume at a price.

Spike, or Ian, next asked Simon Watson Taylor, with whom I was sharing a basement flat near the Fulham Road, after the temporary collapse of my first marriage, if he would allow his premises to be turned into a cinema. Simon, ex-secretary of the Surrealist Group in this country, anarchist and later a prominent adept of pataphysics, the science of imaginary solutions, who savoured anything which proved the hypocrisy of the Establishment, also said yes.

The evening, as you may have guessed by now, was a showing of the history of cinematic porn from late-Victorian days to what was then the present. Simon's only demand was that Mick and I were to join the timber merchants. I found the whole programme fascinating but unarousing, the earliest examples especially. There, with a photographer's rather wobbly period backcloth and the ubiquitous potted palm-tree which often appeared in straight family portraits of that era, were a series of men wearing false beards who had their speeded-up way with women, with both sexes frequently dressed as monks or nuns. (Towards the end of Joyce's *Ulysses* there is a list of the contents of Leopold Bloom's bureau drawers, including several photographs of similar images.)

It occurs to me that pornography, to work, must be contemporary. So many of these monks and nuns, and probably those taking part in the decades that followed, were performers who are long dust – not in any way a turn-on, at least for me.

There was one film, made not long ago (but a week can be a long time in pornography), which showed a woman in the country who sees a man approaching and pretends to faint in the heather by the side of the path, having first carefully disarranged her clothing. The man, spotting her as she intended, takes advantage of her, or vice versa – comic rather than wank-material. The inspector, in his neutral policeman's voice, pitched as though reading a charge, told us, 'She's in Holloway. He's in the Scrubs.'

The final film was more or less contemporary. It showed a fairly established film starlet (presumably 'resting' at the time) and a fairly attractive young man. Simon observed, as he would, that she had a well-developed pile.

But it was a movie he showed earlier that he claimed to be 'the best we have – French', which indeed proved to be the most imaginative and surrealist in the proper sense. A young girl, just before Christmas, indulges in aggressive lesbian horseplay with her governess. Once she is left alone, down the chimney, to her surprise, comes Santa Claus, wearing a carboard mask. Making a magician's pass, he materializes an enormous paper parcel. She eagerly unwraps it to discover a full-size vaulting horse only with a handle on one side, to manipulate back and forth a large model penis at the end. After only a short hesitation, the girl hauls up her nightdress and makes full use of it. A winged female angel appears and engages the attentions of the be-masked Father Christmas. Her wings fall off, and . . . After all have climaxed, the last shot of the film is of the angel's bottom with the discarded mask of Father Christmas placed on it.

When it all finished, having presumably been paid for by Spike (I imagine the detective gave a good share of it to his cameraman and a smaller amount to the uniformed copper in the kitchen), the timber merchants left happy, full of cheese sandwiches and belching bottled beer, and the party was over. Before following in their unsteady wake, the inspector hinted to me and Simon that if we could get together a suitable unisex cast-list, he would be delighted to attend. Without talking it over, we both thought this would be carrying our association with the law too far. We politely declined and Simon went to unpin the 'screen'.

Some time later Simon told this tale to a man he knew but hadn't realized was a runner for *Private Eye*, where it duly appeared, Simon's name and all. He was furious because not only could he have been charged with participation in an illegal activity, but, as he was still working for an airline, he might well have been sacked. In the event no action was taken, although much later and not necessarily involving our three representatives of the law, members of the Vice Squad were accused, charged and convicted of serious offences.

It was all so long ago anyway, years before the Chatterley case, let alone the Beatles' first LP. By now surely the constabulary involved have presumably joined most of the cast, especially the Edwardian religious persons, in grave or urn.

As for Ian's memorial lunch, it's held in either November or early December in a club off the Strand. We meet at the bar. The walls of the big room off it, where we eat at long tables, are hung, unlike those of the Palace with its hand-painted monarchs, with portraits of the theatre stars of yesteryear. The cutlery and glasses are OK, the décor so unremarkable as to be almost invisible.

Here assemble middle-aged or elderly jazz people. Even Mick Mulligan, an infrequent visitor to the Smoke these days, puts in one of his rare appearances from Bognor Regis. The whole strange but highly pleasurable homage to the late Spike was originally conceived and realized by Ian Christie, a far more tolerant figure now than in his days with Mick. He is still the life and soul of the event today, but I'm not sure how much he runs the practical end of things: booking, rounding up of punters, menus etc., as he was recently in great pain with shingles, which, unlike Dr Johnson's statement that being condemned to be hanged helped 'to concentrate the mind wonderfully', certainly curtailed most other activities.

I can't resist here quoting a happily irrelevant few lines from Coward, from a song called 'And That is the End of the News', his reaction to an order from the Labour government after the war for the BBC to lighten up their newscast after so many years of conflict and tragedy:

> Hey ho. Derry down diddle
> Doris's shingles have met in the middle
> She's buried in Devon
> And now she's in heaven.
> And that is the end of the News.

By last year's stomp Ian Christie was back on form. His many years as film critic on the *Daily Express* were, I imagine, not his ideal radical perch, but then neither were Flook's satirical swipes at the Establishment, when I was writing the balloons emerging from the mouth of a furry hippo, in the spirit of the *Daily Mail*'s lumpen-suburban political stance.

It is the custom after our three-course lunch (edible, if neither surprising in its set menu nor yet a date to note down in the thin diary of life's gastronomic highlights) for someone to make a speech in praise of our trumpet-blowing chum, with his combination of chutzpah and modesty – he always blew facing *away* from the audience and with a green beret full of holes draped over the bell of his horn.

Ian had performed this loving task several times over the years and as everybody, leaving aside the odd fart or belch, was completely silent except for the laughs, and the speaker had a mike, I could hear most of it which was not of course true of the conversation at lunch itself. There was an astonishing volume of noise so I was as usual reduced to the nod, which would have satisfied the simple needs of the Dickensian Ancient P. and the smile of Carroll's Cheshire Cat. Ian Christie, I have to say, has always proved an admirable orator: crisp, funny and short (this last is a great virtue in those who speak at banquets or memorial services; in fact I think it's the first essential).

One of the great advantages of the Ian Mackintosh Memorial Lunch is that one meets, as is only too rare, those who shared one's youth: although now grey, balding and in many cases fatter, there they are as in a dream. On being asked how we're feeling, our usual answer is most often 'Not too bad'.

I also show up at the funerals, memorial services or meetings of my near-contemporaries. This is not so much for the sake of the departed, although if I loved or admired them I'm glad to have the opportunity to stand up and be counted, but principally because those present tend to be old acquaintances too, whom I seldom or never see in other circumstances. Thus, in cemetery, graveyard, chapel, public hall or public house, I find myself in touch with different segments of my diverse life: writers, painters, journalists or jazzbos, as the case may be.

Quite recently, at David Sylvester's last exit, an event arranged in advance by him down to the drapery over the coffin (a valuable old weaving removed, I heard later, before he slid into the furnace; but that was after we'd all gone, in my case groping for cigarettes and lighter, into the open air). We stood about for a bit and then, unexpectedly, I was greeted by a healthy-looking, well-preserved man with a moustache, dressed like an Edwardian country squire. He turned out to be the artist John Craxton, whom I'd known and liked very much when I'd worked at the London Gallery in the late forties. I was mildly apprehensive, as I hadn't been too kind about his neo-romantic Greek fishing lads with slight cubist-scaffolding and seductive colour to prove their modernity, and especially in contrast to his then friend Lucian Freud.

John soon set my mind at rest. 'Loved *Don't Tell Sybil*,' he said. 'Haven't laughed so much for ages!'

I was relieved, but you can never tell how people you write about are going to react. A year or two ago (or perhaps much longer, I've completely lost my sense of time) I was in the Lefevre Gallery in Bruton Street at a private view of paintings by Edward Burra (they were his lifelong dealers and friends) when in through the door minced a beautifully dressed, cleverly made-up elderly queen I knew in my bell-bottom days. Glancing at the Burras – he knew very little about pictures – he asked me, not that he cared, 'Are these any good?' He told me next that he and John Trafford, his friend and later another lover of mine, loved my book *Rum, Bum and Concertina*, but how could I remember so much and (indignantly) why had I changed their names! Well, as Fats Waller once said, 'One never knows, do one?'

Another 'must' event concerns 'the Brothers'. I first heard of this organization through my dear friend the piano-player Ron Rubin, a fellow Liverpudlian whom I've known for getting on almost sixty years. He is nearly as deaf as I am, but hates wearing hearing-aids. In consequence he has given up noisy circumstances, including 'the Brothers' and pubs. He has a great dislike of techno piped music.

So, idle as ever, I didn't pursue the organization until gently propelled by Mike Pointon, my Jiminy Cricket when it comes to making me stir my stumps.

I have known and worked with Mike for quite a number of years. I got to meet him when he added his expertise to that of a very nice large radio and documentary maker called Neil. Unlike his partner who knows little of jazz, Mike, small and active, had helped by suggesting suitable subjects and finding the recordings, mostly from his own collection. He sometimes writes the scripts too, although I usually personalize them a little, and he is a great help with the editing. The firm is now self-contained and is called Spools Out (geddit?).

I went on two occasions to the States with the pair of them to make programmes for BBC2 (our main commissioner): covering those cities where jazz perched and developed at different times, from New Orleans to Memphis, and on the second one to case Harlem. They asked me to make a third visit, but I can't cross the Atlantic, much to my sorrow, any more. This is because, having examined my medical records, the insurance company wanted at least four thousand pounds to insure me and the BBC said no way.

So they went by themselves and I helped when I could when they got back and did the narration.

In the States I interviewed several old, some *very* old jazz- and bluesmen, sitting as a rule in rooms stuffed with furniture and in front of enormous television sets. Here Mike provided me with a crib about their careers, hit recordings etc. 'My, my,' said one old boy, 'you sho' done yo' homework!' We also interviewed the keeper of archives and some jazz historians.

The climax of the whole double-whammy for me was being shown the room where Bessie Smith died by the owner of what is now a hotel but was the Colored Hospital, Clarksdale, Mississippi. In a sense it rounded off my long-time obsession with the Empress of the Blues, from that first recording I heard in a study at Stowe in the middle forties to the motel bedroom in ol' Miss a few years back.

Mike and I have much else in common besides an interest in jazz. He is a British music-hall enthusiast and so am I, and the same applies to the early cinema from *Rescued by Rover* onwards. He is currently appalled and enraged by those who remove original soundtracks and have others composed. The British Film Institute, believed to be the guardians of the medium's history, are to be especially reproached. Dalí and Buñuel's surrealist masterpiece, *The Andalusian Dog*, is a case in point. They wiped off the period music, very much part of its makers' intentions, and replaced it by a pretentious load of fly-shit (jazz term for written-down notes). Now, Mike has heard that *Dreams That Money Can Buy*, a post-war film featuring contributions from Hans Richter, Marcel Duchamp, Man Ray, Max Ernst and Fernand Leger, with music by Milhaud and John Cage, has a new score, recently performed at the National Film Theatre. Why, and for whose benefit? Is it an attempt to win over 'youf', of whom there are now fewer than the middle-aged and us oldies? Anyway Mike and I think it (to quote Mr Groucher from *Toy Town*) 'Disgrrraceful!'

And I am equally up in arms at the remake of classic movies. To what end is this activity, apart from for engaging contemporary stars? Most of the remakes are inferior to the originals and tend to 'bomb' anyway. End of grumpy old man explosion.

Mike and I also find the same things funny. In a supermarket in the South he discovered an American version of pepperoni. It was called 'a spicy meat-stick', which struck us both as very camp. It still does, and when we meet both of us assume old-style gay voices and mannerisms for the purpose. 'Have you had your spicy meat-stick this morning?' we ask each other, and a reference to it proves frequently appropriate.

Later, in the same deep-South environment, I noticed a brand of chewing-gum called 'Gummo'. This too was absorbed into our Julian Clary routine: 'Do you like your "gummo" before or after your spicy meat-stick?' we enquire.

Oh, just for the record, Mike is in no way gay.

It was Mike who introduced me to the Brothers, then convening for the last time at 100 Oxford Street with its myths and ghosts. The members are very much the same as those at the Macintosh shindig: middle-aged and old jazzers with a few younger jazz archaeologists.

What the Brothers do is reminisce and drink. When you become a Brother, you get up on the stage (Louis played on that stage), roll up one of your trouser legs and stand on one leg. This sounds very Masonic, but it isn't. Admittedly the foundations of the institution in the US had some connection with religion, but here there is no question of it, and if there had been I for one wouldn't have joined. God ('dog' spelt backwards) has never made us stand on one leg in this country, thank Dog.

Nothing else to it? Not really. It's just a chance to renew old friendships and get a bit one-legless.

Oh, by the way, that versatile Mike Pointon also plays that 'ole slard trombone – and well, too!

The Nicolson Toynbee Lunch was started long, long ago by Benedict Nicolson, not the son of that difficult but accomplished if over-genteel abstract painter of St Ives, but of Sir Harold and his wife Vita Sackville West. Ben himself, a tall and gentle man, was for a long time the editor of *The Connoisseur*. Aside from having a wide knowledge of antiques, he was sociable and founded these monthly get-togethers to promote good company, hopefully intelligent and interesting conversation, and edible food and drinkable wine. Ever since Ben invited me to join, the lunch has taken place in various restaurants, but all of them in Soho, north or south. It now meets in a rather good Italian establishment in Greek Street in an upstairs room with a bar. Numbers vary but are always respectable. This is in part due to the young whipper-in called Anthony Marreco.

When Ben asked me to join the table I was one of the youngest members. Never no more. Some are slightly younger than I, some my age, a very few, looking depressingly young, have already turned eighty.

Several previous members have 'left the table'; Professor Freddie Ayer, for example. Others I haven't seen for a long time, but don't know if they're quick or dead. Manny Litvinoff, for instance, a fine poet and brother of that outrageous and very funny chancer, David.

Unlike his brother, David would never have been invited to attend the Nicolson lunch. He loved risk and danger. He was once in trouble with the Krays, for example, and claimed (truth or no?) that they hung him out of a window by his ankles while a CND march (including me perhaps?) passed underneath. He walked with me once through Soho and kept reaching up to sills and flat surfaces to feel if a metal bar was still in place for emergencies.

He lived for a long time in Tim Whidbourne's large house, then 'the wrong end' of Cheyne Walk, where Victoria and I shared a basement flat with Andy Garnett, and David came down very strictly to get the rent, part of the gas bill etc.

A jazz lover when I first met him, he moved into the early rock world for the excitement and mingled a lot with Mick Jagger in particular. Indeed he was a consultant on the film *Performance* (for his knowledge of the criminal *and* the contemporary and outrageous music world) but even then he loved the old twenties blues and jazz singer Ma Rainey, preferring her comparative primitive performances to Bessie Smith's, her protégée, or anyone else.

Andy and I were once driving to a mill belonging to his formidable mother (who was mercifully absent) to fulfil some service and we took David with us. Andy was at that point fascinated not only by the Chelsea set but also by villains. David was essentially a city ne'er-do-well and was amazed when we finished up in, I think, Berkshire. 'This grass,' he said with stupefied amazement, 'it must be worth something!' His knowledge of nature was non-existent. He called all birds, including sparrows, ducks!

David was gay, in a non-camp way and, although technically rather ugly, his vitality and humour, his *boldness*, won him many rather good-looking partners. He was painted by Lucian Freud, a fine portrait which the artist entitled *The Procurer*. Lucian was, and still is, famous for suing people who assume things, whether true or not, but this time it was David who put the boot in. I don't remember if he won or if it was settled out of court, but it was amazing he did it at all.

After many shared japes – David was absurdly inventive and the master of chutzpah – he vanished from sight. Then I heard he was living in Wales. Why? Were the mob after him? Nobody knows. Shortly afterwards he committed suicide. Again, a mystery; David Litvinoff, an enigma to the end.

Incidentally, it is always an all-male occasion, except the Christmas meeting, when you can bring a 'lady guest', as some of the more elderly members would probably describe a female partner. You can, however, if you warn the secretary in advance, bring a male friend (or partner!) any time.

That noise, like several kettles on the hob, is feminists' blood boiling. I myself can think of lots of women who would enliven the ambience – Germaine Greer for one – but I don't believe that most of the members' wives or 'partners' would enjoy it much, especially as the conversation these days, when I can hear it, is, as per usual with elderly men, mostly pure reminiscence.

I must admit to enjoying these non-PC events. When I was young and thought very occasionally about old age and death (after my grandfather had died in the thirties or my father in the sixties), I used to restore my optimistic equilibrium by reflecting that everyone in the world was for it, and not just golden lads and lasses, but *everybody*!

> Oh dark, dark, dark. They all go into the dark . . .
> The captains, merchant bankers, eminent men of letters
> The generous patrons of the arts, the statesmen and the
>   rulers
> Distinguished civil servants, chairmen of many committees
>   Industrial lords and petty contractors, all go into the
>   dark . . .
>   'East Coker III' – T. S. Eliot

And so we do, including all those who attend the Nicolson and Toynbee Lunch Club.

And who is and who isn't dead, I mean here and now? Sometimes I meet people I thought were dead and they're not. Sometimes I believe people are alive and find out they're not; and, the worst, I imagine I see them in the street and it's not them at all, it's just a stranger who looks a bit like them, but only a bit.

There's an old joke, and you can't stop me if you've heard it, but feel free to groan if that's the case. An old gentleman, on waking up, would read the obituary column in *The Times*. 'And if I'm not in it,' he'd explain to people, 'I get up.'

The Ben Nicolson and Philip Toynbee Lunch was not always so named. When Ben asked me to join, it was simply called the Luncheon Club, but when Ben died it was renamed in his memory and later Philip Toynbee joined him. No need in either of these cases to read the obituary column. If your name is part of the Luncheon Club's full title, it would seem you've left the building.

In fact I didn't know Philip all that well and don't think he was ever present at a lunch I went to, and yet I feel that if he had been there I'd have registered the fact. He was not someone whose presence anywhere you'd forget.

A knowledgeable Bohemian whose father was Arnold Toynbee, the distinguished historian, Philip had become a presence at both posh and louche parties. He was well known at the fashionable Gargoyle club, swaying across the floor under the original Matisse paintings, but he wasn't only quite pissed, he was also extremely promiscuous. If he was at a party and hadn't scored he would, his first wife, Ann, said, walk pathetically round the room asking any young woman not obviously bespoke, 'Will you sleep with me? Will you sleep with me?'

Ann died recently of cancer in great pain but, typically, for she was a remarkable woman, without fuss. I doubt her marriage to Philip was happy, but she was very funny about him after he'd gone. He was very keen on fly-fishing, a brownie point as far as I'm concerned. One day a gust of wind planted his fly in his lower lip. As the fly was barbed and to remove it would mean leaving the water to visit the nearest hospital, he refused to go then, or indeed attend one for several days, and walked around with it stuck there. Ann said it looked truly repellent and that he quite enjoyed the disgust it provoked.

He had two children with Ann, both girls. The elder was called Josephine, ginger-haired and socially rather gauche. She adored Philip. When she in turn was dying, she became, almost overnight, gentle and lovable.

She'd had a child, a beautiful little boy called Pip, whose father was Mexican. Ann adored Pip. When he went to stay with her in her holiday cottage in the west of Ireland, the walls had become brown with peat smoke and Pip thought it was chocolate and tried to lick it off. He must be quite grown-up by now, but I have heard nothing of him lately.

The younger daughter was Polly. Unlike her older sister, she was only a toddler when Ann and Philip broke up. She has therefore no strong feelings about him, whereas Josephine worshipped him. Polly is now an oft-quoted political journalist on the *Guardian* and is frequently on TV panels vigorously defending positive liberalism (small 'l'), but in the days when we still had the Tower near Brecon, she was living just up the road with the ever-smiling documentary TV writer Jeremy Sandford in a pretty but near-slum period farmhouse. His most celebrated play was the influential *Cathy Come Home*, a devastating attack on heartless officialdom, and the walls in their house were collaged with favourable newspaper cuttings.

Polly's father, Philip, was there with a couple of friends the day Polly asked us to lunch. It was held in the large yard in front of the house. The yard itself was reasonably clean in comparison, as Jeremy bred horses.

It turned out to be a magical afternoon. There was a white mist on the hills, but it was warm and you could tell the sun would eventually lift it. Before this happened several of his beautiful equine creatures materialized like phantoms, clip-clopped across the yard and vanished again through another open gate on to the still invisible hill.

Philip was in sparkling form. We talked about fishing for a while, but then he told me he was thinking of giving it up in favour of sailing. He said, 'Every decade one should change one's hobby.' I didn't agree at all with this sub-Cyril Connolly-like aphorism, but I let it go. I only hoped he didn't end up getting a sheet anchor hooked in his lip.

There was only one unfortunate incident in this golden day, and it demonstrated what I'd always heard, that Philip tended to be totally self-centred like a clever toddler. Polly, knowing perhaps from Ann that her father's favourite food was brawn, had managed to get some. In Lancashire or Scotland there'd have been no difficulty, but in Wales over thirty years ago there was none, not even in the huge covered market which is a treasure-house of most fodder. Still, somehow she succeeded and put it in front of Philip in a bowl, expecting no doubt some positive response. Without breaking off his conversation with Jeremy he briefly told his daughter that he no longer enjoyed it. Naturally she was exasperated and upset. Luckily I had a passion for it, inherited from my father like so much else, and I asked if I could gobble it down. She probably thought I said this to save her feelings, but she was at least able to avoid a shout-up. There was also plenty to drink, which helped.

Philip was quite attractive in a rather odd way. He wrote good biographical books which the critics praised, but as they were in verse the public didn't buy them and there are several still not published. He is missed by many people, all of whom fell under his spell. He died, not old, and now shares with Ben Nicolson the full name of the monthly lunch.

Of my three treats the *Oldie* lunches are perhaps, but only just, my favourite. They are held at regular intervals at

'We talked about fishing . . . he told me, "Every decade one should change one's hobby." I didn't agree at all'

Simpson's in the Strand, a famous large old restaurant, unspoilt since the days when Edwardian city gents tucked their napkins over their often formidable stomachs.

It is renowned for its huge joints, carried by waiters on silver-plated dishes covered by hinged domes which they open to get at the splendidly rare meat. The vegetables, on the other hand, roast potatoes apart, are usually dismissed as overcooked, but not by me – I'm no lover of *al dente*.

The lunches are served at long tables and there is a chart outside showing where you'll sit. Against the wall, on a low stage, is the top table and there, with whomever else he decides to sit, is the head Oldie himself, Richard Ingrams.

Ingrams was the founder with several school chums and others of *Private Eye*, in some ways admirable, in others an odious magazine. Grubby-looking but strangely endearing in private, he was the Torquemada, the scourge of Britain, especially in the 'Swinging Sixties'.

He was much admired for printing stories most journalists knew were true but didn't dare touch for fear of legal reprisal. *Private Eye* didn't hesitate to blow it and indeed was frequently sued, most famously by Sir James Goldsmith, the magazine's 'Golden Balls', who won enormous damages. The amount would have bankrupted most journals, but *Private Eye* typically started the 'Golden Balls' fund and enough readers who disliked and mistrusted Sir James, knighted by Harold Wilson in his dubious and mysterious final 'Violet' Honours list, raised enough for the magazine to remain afloat.

Someone who attended part of the trial said that during it 'Jimmy and Ingrams seemed to fall in love with each other'. If they did, it was probably because they were both pirates – very different pirates, but pirates nevertheless. Sir James (like Captain Hook, an old Etonian) was a swashbuckler, a high-stakes gambler, an enthusiastic adulterer. Ingrams, on the contrary, was a puritan, very funny perhaps, but determined to fight the good fight. Both Richard and Jimmy (whom I did meet several times, always feeling like a rabbit caught in the headlights of a Rolls) had powerful charisma.

Those who mistrusted and disliked the *Eye* accused it with some justification of being anti-gay, anti-Semitic and anti-sexual. It was at times all three, but some people made too much of it.

Among other strips it ran one drawn by the ever-inventive Heath and called 'the Sads' (*Private Eye*-speak for gays). One I specially remember showed two shaven-headed, black-leathered, moustached butch frequenters of Old Compton Street. An old-fashioned, wasp-waisted and discreetly made-up old queen minces up to the lads in the pub to tell them how fortunate they are. 'In my day,' he lisped, 'you were constantly threatened by the law, open to blackmail, beaten-up and insulted . . .' In the final frame, one butch sad turns to the other and says, 'Lucky old sod!' Today, in fact, although the police seem to have cooled it, there's still plenty of 'queer bashing' and open insults, and I loathe all that, but then I was gay until I was about thirty.

Anti-Semitism? *Private Eye*? Well, I suppose if you're really PC, Jewish jokes are anti-Semitic, but not to Jews, or at least not to most Jews. My mother, who was Jewish (which means that by Jewish law I am too), loved Jewish jokes, and if I heard a new one I'd ring her to tell her. So when *Private Eye* renamed Weidenfeld & Nicolson 'Snipcock and Tweed', I thought that was both clever *and* funny.

In other respects, however, *Private Eye* was very suspect. From the indiscretions let drop at the famous lunches at the Coach and Horses in Soho, and especially those revealed ('shtrictly between ush) by stupid politicians plied with drink, they gleaned rich pickings, while Nigel Dempster, a famous and much-feared gossip columnist, let them have endless stories he couldn't have used in the *Daily Mail*.

Now most politicians are fair game, but not, I think, when the magazine blew the cover of adulterers, even politicians. Enjoyable for us the readers, of course, but it could break up previously seemingly happy marriages and break hearts too, and, worst, destroy whole families.

Alan Brien, a very good journalist famous at that time, wrote a damning condemnation of this practice, accusing the *Eye* of sending the victims' children 'weeping home from school'. Ingrams's defence was 'Well they [the adulterers] shouldn't have broken their wedding vows anyway!' Puritanical Christian wanker!

He and his confederates seemed not to care that they were causing misery. They started, for example, a column on 'Doctor Jonathan', a pastiche of Boswell's *Life of Dr Johnson*, aimed at J. Miller. It was cleverly done in eighteenth-century mode. Miller (who is a real doctor, of course) is depicted as a smug, over-loquacious, self-praising know-all.

Now there is some truth in this, but Jonathan is also a genuinely creative and original man, whose achievements in so many fields are touched by genius. Yet he is still at his age tortured by insecurity. This comes, I think, from a constant 'pull baker – pull devil' conflict in his nature. His father was a famous psychoanalyst, entirely serious, and had justified hopes that his son might become a medical scientist and make important discoveries. So, indeed, Jonathan eventually became a doctor, working for a time as a GP, but while at Cambridge he had appeared very successfully on the undergraduate stage and eventually in *Beyond the Fringe*, which, via the Edinburgh Fringe itself, became a worldwide success, and so the 'pull doctor – pull actor' conflict began.

My own instinctive reaction is that if you choose, as he for the most part has, to wear the cap and bells, you have to accept you'll find yourself at times in the stocks with the critics throwing dead cats at you. But, in defending himself, he often digs his own bear-pit. His work alone defends him, in theatre and opera direction all over the world, in documentaries both serious and comic, in the anatomizing of a corpse on TV and in the creation of a pop-up book of anatomy (were the last two unconscious nods towards his father?), as an essayist, as a lecturer and collage maker/sculptor; and the critics, some of them at least, have increasingly (as he puts it) 'understood at last'. He needs, he once told me, and it was an odd admission, 'to stand in a Niagara of praise'. Well, tough tit, but I have always loved him, and hated him suffering from the triumphant mockery of minor public-school bullies.

Incidentally, I too appeared in the 'Doctor Jonathan' spoof as 'a critick and voluptuary', although I contributed nothing beyond belching and farting. It didn't worry me, but then a lesson that 'the good doctor', as they called him, has never taken in is that bullies at any age and of any class recognize the poor sod who is sensitive and therefore go for him (or her).

*

Yet *Private Eye* did run certain series which surely even its critics could enjoy. *Mrs Wilson's Diary* was one and the *Dear Bill* letters, correspondence written by Denis Thatcher to a boozy, golf-playing chum, another. Mad, but somehow believable fantasies, they both became popular plays. Indeed Mrs Thatcher, to prove her sense of humour, attended her mauling, and was made so angry, probably by its truth, that she did a Queen Victoria. Had she been Queen, and she often gave the impression she was, she'd have charged Ingrams and the late John Wells, his side-kick, with *lèse-majesté*. She seems to have had no humour at all. Anyway, as an anarchist I rejoiced, and anyway, like *almost* all politicians, she was fair game.

Ingrams, in his pious persona, much admired Malcolm Muggeridge after he'd become religious and, following what black people in the American jazz world call 'turning', had decided that the Lord should make him chaste there and then. For his part, Muggeridge made sure that everybody knew. And indeed the Lord favoured him, dear boy. He gave up booze, fags and women, 'just like that'.

Wally 'Trog' Fawkes, who had loved and continued to love Muggeridge, and I, who couldn't altogether resist his unaltered charm either, introduced into a 'Flook' story a medieval monk called St Mug, who had forsworn all the pleasures of the flesh except in private. Grossly unfair, perhaps, but many irritated by his public piety were very amused, and he became St Mug in everyday conversation and even the press.

Personally, though, I couldn't take Muggeridge's total admiration for Mother Teresa about whom he made a documentary, polishing her halo. I've no time for Mother T at all. My impression, not unsupported by evidence, is that while she showed great compassion for the dying poor of India she showed no interest at all in the conditions which had made them poor in the first place. When, but only when, they were terminally ill, would she open the gates of her hospice and, once her new patients were inside, would shut out the filthy slums outside. Looking at St Mug's documentary and whenever else she's appeared on film or in print, I think that she was a serious backer into the limelight, and I'm probably in a minority there – but I know the signs.

And then Ingrams wrote an admiring biography of Muggeridge, Mother T and all! No, as editor of the *Eye*, Richard Ingrams was a strange and, it seemed to me, quite a sinister figure . . .

But then . . . Ingrams resigned as editor of *Private Eye* and re-emerged as an 'oldie', who organized lunches and started a magazine of that name which published excellent writers who are no longer, or never have been 'hot' (although I suppose these days one is obliged to say 'cool'). The mag is for me one of the most enjoyable publications of our day. Simultaneously he has become a mild and sociable fellow, broadminded as far as I can judge, and convincingly friendly.

I don't know who waved the magic wand to effect this transformation. I can't but wonder whether, if he were still editor of the *Eye* and an explanation for such a transformation about someone came to his ears, he would have published it. No doubt he would, but the change in this case has proved entirely beneficent. He's become a pussy-cat!

The Oldie (a new issue has just arrived in the post) covers a wide field, 'something for everyone', as they used to say.

Richard edits a funny and sharp editorial and also writes a piece on telly, and, among others, there's Miles Kington on books and Dr Stuttaford on the health of 'Senior Citizens', as he mercifully doesn't call them. Memorial Services by Ned Sherrin (relevant to us all), and so on. There is a page divided into two, the top half God, the bottom Mammon. These are all reviews, but there are also features, some regular – there is, for example, a beautiful essay on 'Unwrecked England' by Candida Lycett Green, daughter of the late John Betjeman.

But for me, as an almost retired raver, my top favourite is a piece by what the mag calls this week, 'the loathsome scrounger' Wilfred De'Ath, a wonderful and, given where it appears, a suitable name indeed. The name itself, though, wasn't unknown to me. Outside Victoria station there is a crescent of shops, one of which was called Henry De'ath, the second name painted without much differentiation between the De and the ath, and then, beneath it, 'Family Butcher'. Loved that, real black humour, I thought.

Wilfred presents himself as a penniless ex-lecher living off his wits. He offends some who even write to tell the editor that they will no longer subscribe, but others, like me, are ardent fans. And then one day on the northern-bound train en route for a gig, I got into conversation with a neatly bearded man dressed in a reasonable suit. As he got out, I asked him his name and he told me, 'Wilfred De'Ath'. You could have knocked me down with a zimmer frame. If his self-portrait is accurate then, like the late Jeff Bernard (although I doubt as well paid), he turns his life as 'a loath-some scrounger' into a very funny picaresque chronicle.

There are very funny cartoons in the *Oldie* too, e.g. a

gravestone. At the top is engraved 'R. JONES (M.D.) R.I.P.' and below 'L. JONES (Mrs.) (under the doctor).'

Well, if that isn't a plug – and nobody from the magazine even bothered to bribe me – I don't know what is.

Not all the many people at the *Oldie* lunches are old. There were, for instance, people like my ex-neighbour, Anna Hay-craft, who has now left the building and wrote well-reviewed, rather sour but clever novels under the pen-name Alice Thomas Ellis. She was an excellent cook herself but often, when I saw her at it, she had a cigarette in her mouth over the stew she was stirring.

She was a devout Catholic, and at one time wrote the 'God' column in the *Oldie*. God, if He exists, didn't look after her, or perhaps He was just testing her à la Job. One of her young fell off a roof and was in a coma as a result, from which, though a long time later, he died. I hope her religion helped her. It was a terrible thing to happen and he was such a nice boy.

One of Anna's close chums was the writer Beryl Bain-bridge. I love Beryl who, in that she is a Liverpudlian, earns an extra bonus. She covers the theatre in the magazine, but also writes amazing novels. Her early books tended to be based on Merseyside, but more recently she has chosen famous moments in history, but from an unexpected angle and giving the reader an extraordinary sensation of being there as if in a time warp.

She is also a legendary boozer, although you'd never guess so from her crystalline prose, and she smokes non-stop (although I heard a rumour that she is trying to give up). Once, at a literary thrash, I noticed I had been left alone with her. When, only a little later, I helped her get to her feet again after she'd fallen into a mercifully unlit fireplace, I began to understand why.

I found myself obliged to pour her into a taxi and accompany her to a mainline station to catch a train to, as far as I can remember, Dorking, to address her publisher's salesmen, as writers are obliged to with a new book on the stocks. Somehow I put her on the train. I can't imagine what she told the travelling book salesmen.

But some of the *Oldie* diners *are* old, and some *very* old. Until he 'left the building', Spike Milligan was most often there, on his final visit assisted by his new wife-cum-nurse, a clearly sweet-natured blonde (and she must bloody well have had to be).

He was visibly dropping to bits, clearly close to dying, looking like what my mother called 'death warmed up'. Especially with his pretty carer, he looked like 'Young Mr Grace' in *Are You Being Served?*

Indeed, he went soon after. He'd been a remarkable man, seriously hampered by being a manic-depressive, but certainly a comic genius to whose spring of creative invention most worthwhile post-war British humour owes its origin.

Sometimes he and I got on, sometimes we didn't. When I was TV critic for the *Observer*, I covered a documentary made with Spike's co-operation about his mental illness. In it he insisted that the staff of the asylum had *deliberately* given him a room overlooking the yard where at 6 a.m. they brought all the rubbish bins and emptied them into the vans, making the maximum noise to torture him.

Reviewing these sad delusions, I queried his belief that

they housed him there by design to drive him more mad. I did praise him as a comic genius. But the following week I got a furious letter. In it he told me that he'd been up all night trying to persuade a paranoid young man not to commit suicide. 'WHAT HAVE YOU DONE FOR THE FUCKING HUMAN RACE TODAY, MELLY?' he thundered. He also attacked me for calling him a genius. 'Van Gogh was a genius,' he told me. 'I'm *just a comedian!*'

No, Spike you were not *just* a comedian. You were also the author of two best-selling comic novels about the war, a fine actor, and the inspiration of many surreal-minded heirs. Even today, and usually rather irritatingly, people imitate the catchphrases of your grotesques in *The Goon Show*s. Then there is *The Running, Jumping and Standing Still* film (Dick Lester's short but brilliant début is spiked with your spirit), you played in *Treasure Island* at the Mermaid Theatre for many years; while in *Oblomov*, in the leading role, you improvised every night, and the rest of the cast had to ad lib too – nerve-racking, I'd have thought.

No, Spike, you were quite right when you claimed that Van Gogh was a genius but, however angry it made you to be told, so were you.

What is a genius? Who qualifies to be called one? I once asked the philosopher and excellent hoofer Freddy Ayer to define it. 'A genius,' he said, 'is someone who alters, however radically, however slightly, our perception of reality.' That will do me, and supports my assertion that Spike Milligan falls into Freddy's category.

Some years back they made a TV programme around John Chilton's Feetwarmers, with Spike Milligan as the star guest. I was to sing and Spike to read his children's poems, which happen to be my least favourite area of his work. I know the kiddies love them but for me, while showing our shared admiration for Edward Lear, Spike's homage lacks the touching melancholy of that 'Dirty landscape painter who hated his nose' (W. H. Auden). Spike, who loved jazz and wished he'd been skilled enough to play it professionally, also agreed to join Chilton for a couple of numbers.

The evening turned out to be a disaster, as far as Spike was concerned. The usual seemingly half-witted audience were delivered by that worldwide agency prepared to fly them anywhere in the universe (only joking, folks!). They turned out to be friendly, if hardly rapturous, towards the songs and the band, but totally indifferent towards Spike's poems. What they really went for (presumably in illustration of Dr Johnson's assertion that the public will go anywhere to see a dog walking on its hind-legs) was Spike playing with John. They clapped, they shouted for more, and Spike, the rejected poet, the acclaimed jazzbo, came off furious about it – sulky and snappy.

When we'd been planning that show, the director took Spike and me out to lunch. In a fruit bowl on the table was a beautiful green and yellow striped melon. This shifted Spike into his William Blake-ish, idiot-savant gear, another facet I found perfectly resistible. 'How beautiful that melon is,' he started. 'Isn't it a proof that Goddy exists?' ('Goddy' was Spike's equivalent of Blake's 'Noboddy' or Auden's use of 'She'; in his case to enrol God in the ranks of camp belief.)

Less and less as I grow older do I bother to argue with believers unless what they are supporting is really suspect, like forbidding pessaries or divorce – but that melon somehow got to me.

'But if we weren't sitting here,' I began, 'or the melon was in another restaurant or on the vine, we wouldn't see it at all, and couldn't assert that its beauty, about which the melon itself is completely unaware, proved anything at all.'

Spike conceded, but very grumpily. I don't think he'd taken in my argument at all. For him 'Goddy' was still up there. It didn't augur well for the evening ahead.

I think a lot of trouble came, despite his own successes, from his jealousy of the worldwide fame of his fellow Goon, Peter Sellers. Actually Sellers himself was a neurotic, but it did nothing for Spike's own misery.

I can't resist a groan-making Van Gogh joke.

GAUGUIN: Would you like a drink, Vincent?
VAN GOGH: No thanks, Paul, I've got one ear.

At Simpson's, after our rather heavy, but good lunch, Richard calls for silence to introduce the speaker or speakers. There is a mike, so even I can hear. It's usually, but not always, a free plug for authors who've just had, or are about to have, books published, and an entertainment for us elderly punters. If they are amusing, and Richard takes trouble to establish they can be, we, made tolerant from food and drink, laugh like anything.

When that's all over, we slowly drift or hobble away.

These lunches are not only held in London, some are in the provinces: Edinburgh during the Festival, for instance and elsewhere, like Oxford during the book festival, and points north.

But I haven't been to one of those, too much of an effort for an old creaky, so I stick to the Strand. I have, however, been a speaker there when my naval memoirs *Rum, Bum and Concertina* came out. I was quite rude and got a lot of ribald laughter, but at the end a furious and pompous old citizen came and abused me for telling tales out of Stowe. 'You're a disgrace to the school,' he shouted, red-faced and spitting, 'and a disgrace to J. F. Roxburgh.' That was the headmaster, whom, unlike some, I adored. He naturally had faults: he was very snobbish and extremely tactless in his handling of the staff, most of them, in wartime, hauled reluctantly out of retirement. He was also wonderful with the boys, and although he was possibly a repressed homosexual, and was so described by Evelyn Waugh, I don't think, at Stowe at any rate, he ever laid a well-manicured finger on any of the pupils. His ideal, I would say, was a very beautiful, very clever Lord. I was none of these things, but we got along well enough. He called me 'Garje'.

Well, as he appeared in the first chapter of my book, I spoke of him affectionately but lightly. That is particularly what infuriated my red-faced contemporary. 'Insulting J. F.,' he shouted at me several times. There was no reasoning with him, so I told him to piss off and eventually, still cursing and muttering, he did.

I bet J. F. didn't give him six on the bare bum. With me he was in a position where, for scholastic political reasons, he had to. After the beating he told me to jump about in the passage outside his ravishing Gothic quarters and, when it stopped hurting, to come in and have a sherry. Typical of him, but I was lucky I did develop a liking for taking around a bottle of Tio Pepe to the rooms occupied by a dominatrix.

As it happens, I do quite frequently knock back a sherry before we walk or totter in for the excellent *Oldie* luncheon and sparkling speakers put before us by the now admirable, new-born Richard Ingrams.

Simple pleasures, then, all at given intervals, all largely peopled by my own contemporaries. There are other pleasures certainly, events which delight me, sometimes to my surprise – an annual party given by the writer and critic John Gross, to which he invites everybody who has entertained him that year; mixed age groups from the aged George Weidenfeld, my first publisher, to some young and glamorous women, but best of all, auld acquaintances whom I've never brought to mind, but am delighted to see again and to join as we swig a cup of kindness yet. Diana goes to that party and so does Venetia, but then so do many I never ordinarily get in touch with largely due to my indolence. And there are other unexpected treats.

But also there are past pleasures which are no longer available. I'll list them now, certainly regretfully, but in my day I got (and in my memory still do) a great deal of pleasure from them and during a particularly rich period too.

First the theatre. Deafness is my gaoler here. As you have read, when I had my hearing test I could register all the Big Ben notes but nothing over a certain pitch and ski-slope deafness was diagnosed. At first I was delighted with my hearing-aid but gradually I became disillusioned. Cars, lorries and low-flying planes seemed incredibly noisy and, worse, I could hear men or deep-voiced lesbians better than straight women. Ah, I thought to myself, that's why I can hear men and butch dykes, but not quiet, well-spoken women – or even noisy ones. Still, I learn to live with it in ordinary life; but I began to find the theatre impossible.

This didn't happen immediately, I just thought method acting was to blame, but then, as my hearing got worse, I would have had difficulty hearing Sarah Siddons or Bernhardt. Women, you see, always women.

I used to go to the theatre quite often with Venetia and it was with her I finally had to admit defeat. We went to *Les Liaisons Dangereuses*. I knew the book well and was really looking forward to seeing it on the stage, especially as all the critics had spoken well of it. Well, the ski-slope defeated me. I could hear the louche but eventually repentant young man more or less perfectly but when the wicked countess was hatching her evil plots – nothing. It was as if it were either a monologue for him or she was appearing on television with the sound off. I had to own up, I'd had the theatre.

So have I never visited a playhouse again? Musicals, if I want to see them, I can just about handle because the book is often so idiotic it doesn't matter. Then, if I know a play really well, I can follow it from memory. *Macbeth* and *Hamlet*, for example. How right, and in my case useful, was the old lady who'd never been to the theatre before and saw *Hamlet* at her very first visit. Afterwards she said that she hadn't realized Shakespeare was so full of quotations. Above all, though, *Henry IV, Parts 1* and *2* are no trouble at all because when I was still in the Navy I used to come up to London and go to the New Theatre where the Old Vic company were appearing in repertory and – what seemed to me then bad luck – it was always the two Henrys which I caught, oh at least four times. Mind you, as the cast for each play starred Ralph Richardson as Falstaff and Laurence Olivier as Hotspur, I was always enchanted.

Having left school far too early, Diana later decided to take an exam in English Literature to prove she could pass, and *Henry IV* was the set Shakespearian play, so I was constantly asking her the sort of questions she might have to answer and we drove over to Stratford to see it. It never seemed boring to me, however *déjà vu*. I'd always had an ambition to play the old drunken ne'er-do-well, but never did and now I couldn't because I wouldn't be able to hear my cues and certainly not the prompter.

For a long time after the war I saw everything worth seeing – Ken Tynan's reviews in the *Observer* were a great help here: the first production of *Look Back in Anger* for a start, and also most productions at the Royal Court, including Nigel Dennis's *The Making of Moo*, an anti-religious play about the invention of God to keep the natives in one of our colonies quiet. John Osborne himself played the governor, who felt it might be effective to invent some kind of communion – 'Potato crisps and tomato juice' was his suggestion. I saw *Waiting for Godot* several times and, taking a contra-Tynan's, pro-Brechtian stand, Ionesco at the Arts Theatre and all his plays up to *Rhinoceros* (the least good, I felt) and Arthur Miller and early Pinter and Tennessee Williams, and and and . . . If there's a revival of any of these nowadays and I know them well enough I sometimes go to see them with Diana's and my friend Susannah Clapp, the current theatre critic of the *Observer*.

Finally, if I'm at the cottage I quite often go to the famous

Watermill Theatre, a converted mill. (I love Bagnor, our village, because it has a theatre at one end of the small road facing a little stream, and a pub at the other. No church, but also – the one blot on the landscape – no shop, but it's no distance to one on my granny-mobile.)

The Watermill has the advantage of being quite small, with very good acoustics and a kind of halter you put round your neck to make it all louder. It's not perfect but better than my two aids. Besides the theatre often does musicals, and some are so good they tour or transfer. Anyway as a local I feel I should support this admirable and unfunded institution, rather like grandees feel obliged to go to church in the country.

Still the theatre in general is in the past.

So, too, although this may surprise you, is the cinema. Of course, it's loud enough, but I can't manage to grasp what they're booming on about. I can more or less date my escalating deafness from the films I could still hear. They were as recent as *Dirty Harry* or *Desperately Seeking Susan*, but to speak of past films is in itself a boring trap, except when talking to those equally given to nostalgia. Today I don't even know the names or appearances of recent stars, whereas those glamorous creatures whose framed photographs lined the staircases of the Odeon or the Forum still haunt me. I loved *film noir*, horror movies, comedies, especially if they featured W. C. Fields or Laurel and Hardy. I loved the 'dainty teas' they used to provide in the cinema café and even the Hammond organ with its ever-changing coloured lights.

I was for a time the film critic of the *Observer*, after David Astor elevated me from TV, which actually I enjoyed more. It was the beginning of the seventies and so many of the films I saw, not all but a burgeoning majority, were real bummers. Or was it just me casting an over-golden light on the screens of my youth and the Hollywood gods and goddesses who appeared on them? It's possible.

Before leaving the one-and-nines, I must emphasize, as no doubt I have already, that my top favourite director, from his first film, *An Andalusian Dog*, right through to his last, *That Obscure Object of Desire*, is, was and ever will be Luis Buñuel: his lack of sentimentality and absence of stylistic tricks, his consistent black humour, his knowledge of human frailty and frustrated love and their effects, his consistent atheism ('I'm still an atheist, thank God,' he once told a reporter), his knowledge of the evil bred from poverty, his very being. For his sake I'd face the devil (in which he didn't believe and nor do I) himself. He went deaf too and drank too much. I worship him and all his works.

I suppose theatre and cinema are my main losses, or at least those I most regret. I can't walk very far so I don't walk very far. I need a banister, a wall or an arm to go up or down stairs, I forget more and more, and even when it comes to what I used to be able to do – change a fuse or send a fax – something goes wrong. But these are just the inevitable punishments for having lived a long time and also a hedonistic life. I don't regret that at all. I feel pretty good. I've a rich memory bank to draw on and I don't care too much what happened yesterday afternoon.

I'll have a drink now and a fag and then fall up the stairs to bed. I'm going to Brighton tomorrow to attend the unveiling of a statue to its native son, Max Miller – 'No, listen, listen . . .'

Envoi

I strove with none, for none was worth my strife.
Nature I loved, and, next to Nature, Art;
I warmed both hands before the fire of Life;
It sinks, and I am ready to depart.

Walter Savage Landor

I read this poem in an anthology at school. While certainly not great poetry it touched me then and still touches me now. In my case the first line is not completely true – I have striven with a few although not many – but the rest will do. If they so decide (by that time a matter of indifference to me), it would make a suitable conclusion to a memorable bunfight. Perhaps my son Tom, a trained actor after all, could read it. Even so, in itself, it isn't sufficient to end the book.

There are, for one thing, several people whom I have loved, admired or believe have influenced me and yet are either not or very little in evidence in the text. These do not include those who fulfil all the conditions but who I – or if not I, others – have written about at length elsewhere.

Even so, how to celebrate these figures without printing one of those unread lists found in charity programmes or proceeding at breakneck speed after films or TV documentaries? I have been much exercised by the question but an answer came to me when I was reading a book of early poems by John Betjeman and came across one he called

'I'll have a drink now and a fag and then fall up the stairs to bed'

'Dorset' but was itself based on a much older poem by Thomas Hardy celebrating the lives and final resting place of West Country agricultural workers.

Betjeman retains the shape and some of the imagery of the seer of Wessex: Mellstock Churchyard, for instance, and Tranter Reuben, the first of Hardy's list of cadavers. But he substitutes the rest of them with his own contemporaries: T. S. Eliot, Edith Sitwell, Bryan Howard and so on, although he adds a note: 'The names in the last lines of these stanzas are put in not out of malice or satire but merely for their euphony.'

Well, in my version not for euphony, but in celebration. Here then is my contribution. I have decided also to rename it 'Melly's Churchyard' not for vainglory (at least I hope not) but because 'Melly' and 'Mellstock' are so close phonetically.

Melly's Churchyard

George the Fifth, Lloyd George and Kipling, all alive when I
      was born
Soon my pram would cast a shadow on my father's father's
      lawn.
Happy at my kindergarten. Hated 'Parkfield' (hate it now)
While Alan Stocker, Maggi Hambling, Edward Burra, Tony
      Earnshaw, Elda Abramson and Kezzie
Lie in Melly's churchyard now.

In the grounds of Stowe were follies where we'd meet our
      latest crush
While the war raged on in Europe, we slept sound in rural
      hush.

In bell-bottoms, during training, Hitler stepped his filthy row
While Lady Stuart, Gloria Taylor, Robin Banks, and Jimmy
   Rushing, Cleopatra and Django, dear Penelope and Alex
Lie in Melly's churchyard now.

Growing feeble and less active, not much future, lots of past
Can still sing, if I am seated. Cannot wade, but still can cast
Watch them queue to leave the building (shall not hesitate to
   bow)
While William Meadmore, D. Sylvester, dear Louisa, Michael
   Woods, Jack 'Butch' Waring, Diana Melly
Lie in Melly's churchyard now.

See you later!

George Melly

Acknowledgements

With thanks to: Jo Bins, who managed to decipher my handwriting and type everything up; Diana Melly who, in her role as Wing Commander, faxed, printed and bullied me into finishing before my third deadline; Maggi Hambling, who drew the pictures; my editors Tony Lacey and Zelda Turner for waiting so patiently; Harry Borden, the excellent photographer who took the shots for the book jacket; and to Bela Cunha, John Hamilton, Laura Hassan and Bill Hamilton for all their help.